SPATIAL INFRASTRUCTURE

ESSAYS ON ARCHITECTURAL THINKING AS A FORM OF KNOWLEDGE

José Aragüez

Table of Contents

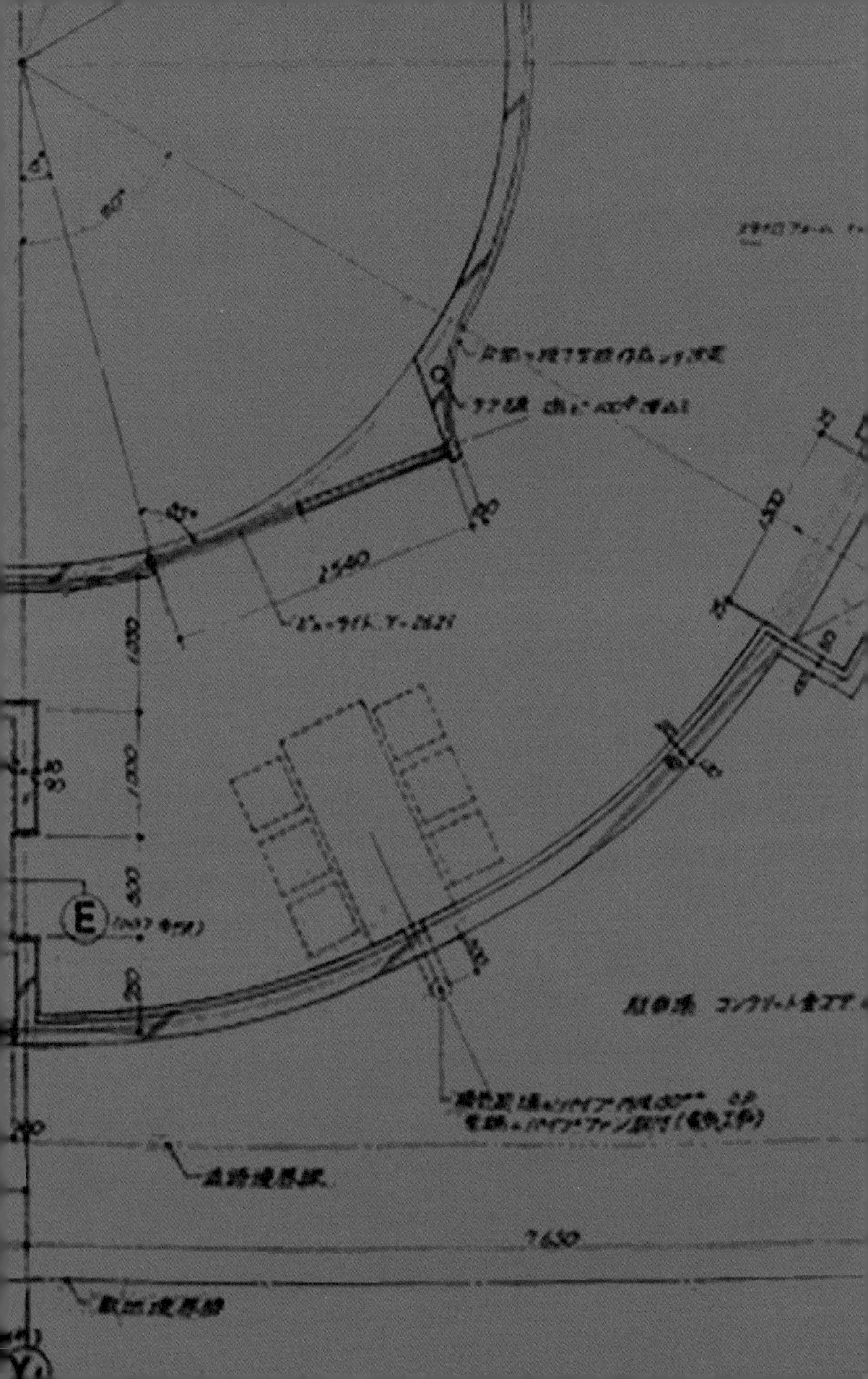
2540
1000
1000
800
E
200

Introduction

Insofar as purposes validate frames of judgment—one cannot judge goalkeepers by how many goals they score, but by how many they stop—a question must always be posed at the beginning of each work as to which field constitutes its target. Is the work an attempt to make a contribution to the discipline(s) to which it belongs, or to other external disciplines? This book falls primarily in the former category, although it also discusses the latter and suggests ways in which that externality can be undertaken while remaining meaningfully grounded in the original discipline(s). Indeed, the main purpose of this project is to make a contribution to architectural thinking—the discursive domain at the heart of the field of architecture—and more precisely, to explore the possibility of recasting architectural thinking as a form of knowledge.

Architectural thinking refers here to the repository of discursive knowledge engendered through the analysis, discussion, and conceptualization of aspects of two inextricably imbricated regimes: that of the building and that of the design process leading to it. In this proposition, the term *discursive* is not utilized in its Foucauldian sense, but rather in its classical connotation, which alludes to the kind of knowledge involving premises, narratives, concepts, ideas, judgments, inferences, conclusions, etc., as channeled through thought and expressed through language. History and theory are both exceptionally potent and essential discursive practices.

Architectural thinking is a specific domain of knowledge, yet by no means is it autonomous. It distinguishes itself from other domains pertaining to design, such as those bound to product, furniture, exhibition, or installation design, urbanism, etc., each of which revolves around a distinct object of knowledge ascertainable through its set of specificities. By extension, architectural thinking sets itself apart from domains external to design, such as biology, sociology, politics, journalism, economics, or media studies, each of which, once again, centers around a clearly identifiable object of knowledge.

While specific, architectural thinking is nonetheless a permeable domain, connected to any number of those other domains and to culture at large. An analogous combination of specificity and non-autonomy is characteristic, for instance, of the main constituents comprising the human body: the eyes possess such a degree of complexity and specificity that they require a specialist of their own, the eye doctor, despite being indissolubly tied to the other constituents of the human organism. Architectural thinking likewise possesses such a rich combination of complexity and specificity that it ought to be considered on its own terms, notwithstanding the links with other domains and the extent to which some of these contribute to its—as well as to each other's—determinations. To choose the example of politics and economics: it is certainly the case that the political and economic circumstances of a particular country, city, or district delineate the realm of possibility in which architecture may or may not take place. But while those circumstances may even have an impact on the characteristics of the architecture that gets built, they do not establish either its fundamental make-up or the totality of its remaining features. In other words, architecture is far from being an epiphenomenon.

Take any competition brief and the entries it prompts. A competition brief is largely the result of the political and economic forces at play in the locale for which it is envisioned. And yet, the entries it obtains might feature entirely different architectural approaches and languages. This is because the threshold between the boundary conditions induced by dynamics external to architecture and the specificities of the artifact is so large that architects still have enough agency over those specificities and their assemblage—often more than they are capable of recognizing—to distinctively define them.

Written over the first fifteen years of my career as an architect and writer, the eight essays selected for this collection mainly seek to tap into and contribute to the multilayered, infinitely nuanced substrate of that threshold, in contradistinction to any of the humanistic and social science domains whose object of knowledge is peripheral to architectural thinking (political theory, ethics, or history of religion, to mention a few). Differently put, these writings aim to fundamentally reassess the combination of specificity and non-autonomy laid out above by thoroughly investigating issues pertaining to architectural thinking, while examining any appropriate scientific, critical, and cultural dimensions wherever sufficiently germane to those issues.

Targeting the Field Itself

In the body of the book, the essays have been chronologically ordered according to year of publication or completion, as the case may be. (Some have been published before, others have not). However, in the interest of the introduction approximating a self-contained piece of writing, here they are presented on the basis of the textual relationships between their synopses, as well as the section heading to which they are most closely related. The first six can be introduced as follows.

For a few decades now, the building has primarily been a means rather than an end in architectural history and theory. **"The Building's Discursive Building"** (2016; pp. 55–67) articulates a theory of the building, in addition to a framework to discuss what it means for one building to embody a significant contribution to the history of architecture in terms of particular design aspects, concepts, and expressive formats relevant to the conception and reading of works in general. From the broader to the more specific approach, the following five essays address that question through a variety of case studies and analyses of both historical and contemporary conditions.

Organicism in architecture betrays its full scope when remaining primarily about visual evocations of the natural world, since the implications of the organic paradigm—involving procedural strategies, relational properties, and constitutive logics—precede questions concerning shape. By examining the philosophical implications of the term "organic" and its intersection with twentieth-century architecture, **"Toward a Critique of 'The Organic' in Architectural Thinking"** (2009–2012; pp. 39–53) argues for an expanded interpretation of the term based on its original definition.

The one-sided approach to form manifest in the history of engineering patents reveals a niche of opportunity for scientific thinking to unleash its unique aptness to facilitating the conception of new models of spatial organization at the building scale. **"Patenting Arrangement"** (2021–2022; pp. 151–165) weaves together a critical analysis of the under-researched domain of patents and the identification of a relatively small subdomain within the tradition of the architecture-engineering hybrid, which unveils an as-yet largely untapped and immense intelligence for growing architectural thinking.

While tending to be tied to the sensory properties of a building relating to its outline or envelope quality, the realm of imageability *as expanded after the so-called "Bilbao Effect" possesses a tremendous potential for catalyzing alternatives to the long-standing duality of* building-as-representation *versus* building-as-spatial-organization *that continues to be pervasive in the field.* **"Critical Imageability"** (2008–2018; pp. 101–127) suggests that the development of design strategies resonating at the level of imageability over the last twenty-five years bears the imprint of their usage exceeding the sphere of signification alone, and argues for conceiving spatial organization through protocols of representation as a way of turning answers to the constant demands on a building's imageability to the disciplinary advantage of architecture.

Works exhibiting a marked uncodedness—i.e., linguistic self-determinacy—transcend received formats of architectural expression and discourse. **"Self-Determinacy via Disciplinary Diversification"** (2010; pp. 15–37) assesses to what extent the student output of The Cooper Union School of Architecture between 1964 and 1985 lived up to the potential for singularity written into the school's teaching methods, and further, how exactly that idiosyncratic potential nurtured a certain adequacy for disruption of the discipline's *status quo*.

A rigorous yet adaptive geometric, structural, and programmatic interpretation of sponge surfaces opens up unprecedented possibilities for architectural design and thinking, beyond the duality of modernism versus postmodernism. **"Sponge Territory"** (2017; pp. 69–79) looks at one single building, the Taichung Opera House designed by Toyo Ito & Associates, and sets out to delineate a new design understanding out of it—in this case, centered around the origination of buildings based upon counter-intuitively simple yet intricate spatial arrangements.

The most central observation that surfaces across these five essays is that there is a correspondence between turning the question of spatial organization into a primary realm of experimentation and innovation, and the possibility of a building embodying a significant contribution to the history of architecture. Indeed, if a building is essentially a three-dimensional, material set of elements distributed in space in such a way that the whole has the capacity to realistically accommodate a collection of human or human-related activities, then it is the specific spatial organization of those elements that confers that whole the basis of its *architecturalness*. In other words, spatial organization lies at the very core of architectural thinking, and therefore an intense focus on it can enable fundamental changes in the manner buildings are devised.

Hence it is no surprise that a significant number of the paradigm shifts taking place across twentieth- and twenty-first-century architecture involved a foundational rethinking of the spatial organization of a building's main elements: from Adolf Loos's *raumplan*, to Frank Lloyd Wright's novel plan layouts and rapports between structure and program; from the free plan to the separation between façade and structure, two of Le Corbusier's five points; from OMA / Rem Koolhaas's free section, to Stan Allen's *field conditions*; from the contributions to housing by MVRDV (Winy Maas, Jacob Van Rijs, and Nathalie de Vries), centered around imaginative three-dimensional dispositions of units, to the topographic distributions of program in concert with surface and structure by Foreign Office Architects (Farshid Moussavi and Alejandro Zaera-Polo); from the bursting of a building's load-bearing structure into minimal components arranged as occupiable clusters, to an unprecedented spatial organization featuring two out-of-phase series of subspaces interweaving in plan and section without ever intersecting, two of

Toyo Ito's most striking inventions. It is the realization of the vital importance of rethinking spatial organization that motivated the construction of a general theory purporting to expand the realm around it, *spatial infrastructure.*

Any spatial infrastructure *embodying a previously unavailable three-dimensional organization extends the bounds of possibility of its conception and realization, and with it those of architectural thinking at large.* **"Spatial Infrastructure"** (2018–2021; pp. 129–149) identifies an elemental material entity that has so far escaped detailed reflection as a recognizable ensemble in buildings, turning it into a new general concept through which to both look at architectural history afresh and envisage future works differently in the pursuit of rational organization channeling—and channeled by—imagination.

Engaging with the Outside through Architectural Specificity

By contributing to the domain of architectural thinking, this book aspires, among other things, to resist the expanding estrangement between architects and historians/theorists. First and foremost, the importance of fostering links between these two aspects of the discipline has to do with the necessity to develop original ideas, arguments, concepts, and narratives from within architecture's own epistemology. For it is this endeavor that uniquely grows the discipline of architecture—a type of growth taken for granted as imperative in most other fields, but strangely not in this discipline, where it often needs to be explicated and even justified in the face of discourse dealing only with subjects beyond its periphery. Indeed, the advancement and progress of the architectural discipline along the lines of its defining specificities should be a *de facto* demand on its historical development, not least given the role of architectural thinking in both shaping and responding to the rapidly changing world of design. In this sense, insofar as architectural thinking is fundamentally a discursive domain, the exercises of history and theory happen to be particularly well suited to broadening the realm of its possibilities.

Further, a solid shared territory between architects and historians/theorists impedes the erosion of—and, in fact, keeps feeding the creation of—discursive planes in which to ground value beyond mere opinion or fad, while preventing the blind, uncritical recycling of past formats of architectural thinking. Concerning practice, discursive energies intensely devoted to architectural thinking may provide fruitful matrixes for design, thereby increasing the levels of sophistication of the architecture being conceived—both as designed artifacts and in regard to how it engages its immediate and extended contexts.

In addition to contributions to the field of architecture itself, of the kind outlined in the section above, links between architects and historians/theorists can also be formed and strengthened via discursive endeavors that engage with domains of knowledge and practice outside of architecture and yet remain firmly rooted in the specificities of architectural thinking. This approach follows in the tradition of figures such as Alan Colquhoun, Robin Evans, Kenneth Frampton, and Stan Allen, and counters the dynamic prevalent today, where external fields are addressed in their own terms from within architectural studies, while nearly all architectural thinking is left behind in the process. There is little doubt that this is one of the main causes behind the divorce between architects and historians/theorists that has been unfolding for almost two decades now in the Anglo-American scene.

Beyond the limitations of both critical and so-called "post-critical" stances, a critical constructionism *would galvanize architecture's destabilizing power to radically rearticulate external domains of experience and signification, and to breed new knowledge of contemporary sociocultural dynamics, rather than merely translate them into its code.* **"On Architecture's Metacriticality"** (2011–2018; pp. 81–99) discusses the lineage of criticality and post-criticality in architecture—with a focus on the American scene—in relation to recent shifts within the larger context of sociocultural theories of critique.

What are the architectural equivalents of systems of thought engendered in other fields that proved capable of exerting a major influence beyond their original disciplinary boundaries, such as Freudian psychoanalysis, Frankfurt School dialectics, and deconstruction? In fact, to what extent has architecture been able to generate comprehensive, fully fledged systems of thought at all? "The Building's Discursive Building," introduced above, ventures ways in which analyzing buildings can precipitate the generation of robust theoretical frameworks, whose impact might extend beyond architecture into other domains of knowledge and practice.

From the broader to the more specific approach, "On Architecture's Meta-criticality" and "The Building's Discursive Building" propose projects where rigorous and in-depth discussions of questions concerning architectural thinking would either be combined with studies of problems, discourses, terms, and events pertaining to fields outside of architecture—insofar as they can be significantly relevant to those questions—or more ambitiously, would serve as a platform from which to substantially affect any number of those external fields.

———

At a time when the architect's commitment to considering the pressing issues of our time—from social justice to equity and climate—is more critical than ever, an engaged disposition will only be truly effective if a deeply informed knowledge of the specificities of the field lies behind it. In that regard, devoting a concerted effort to reexamining the grounds of architectural thinking becomes a necessary exercise precisely because it can yield a meaningful expansion of architecture's agency, from first principles. Indeed, pertinent conceptualizations of what architects do are able to prompt massive changes in building paradigms, and through them, the kinds of transformations in the field's engagement with the world that have the power to make a difference both inside and outside of the field.

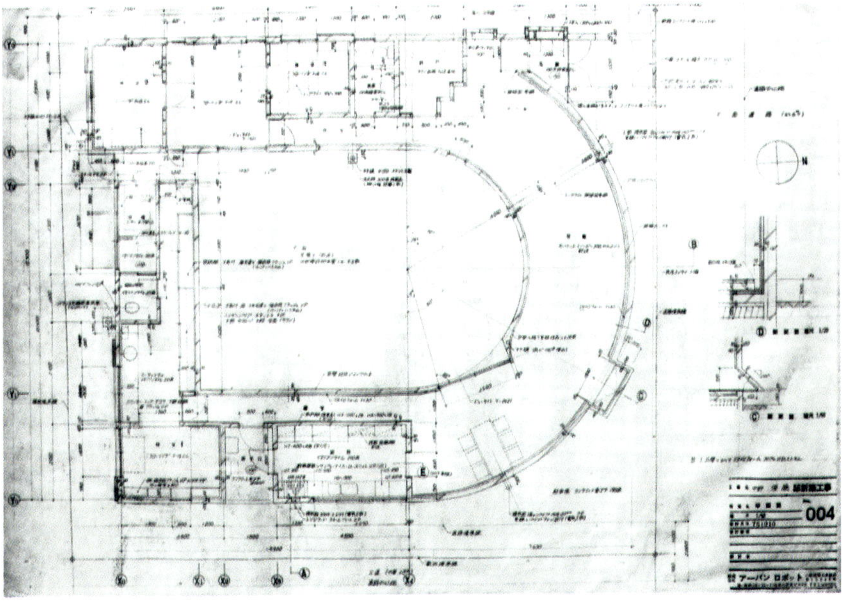

0.1 Toyo Ito. White U House in Tokyo (1975–1976).
Construction drawing, floor plan.

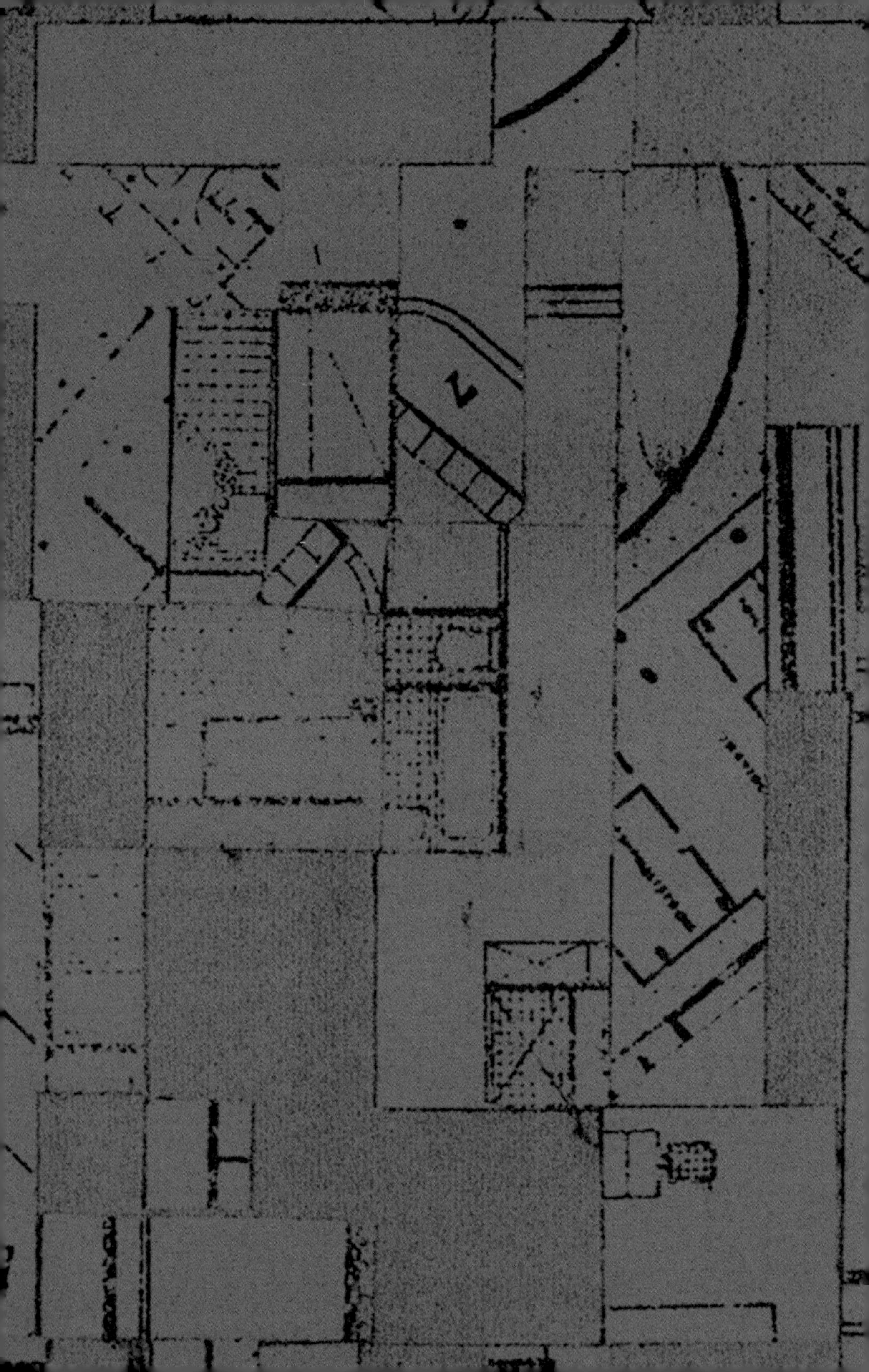

Self-Determinacy via Disciplinary Diversification: The Cooper Union School of Architecture, 1964–1985

> Sometimes you have a difficult time because there is no stimulus. If there are no stimuli you have to create your own stimuli. The sixties was a time when there were a lot of stimuli, right? I mean, in the other disciplines . . . I never go to a gallery to look at painting because I know that there is nothing that inspires me. So, it's a difficult time because sometimes you feel like you live in a vacuum, and you have very few friends with whom you can truly exchange, you know, essential arguments. So, one has to simply accept that one is lonely when one aspires to the ideal of one's own discipline.[1]

The period between the 1960s and the 1980s was particularly fruitful in architecture academia, as various schools around the world contemporaneously housed a series of striking experimental practices relating to the domain of pedagogy. To mention a few examples, the School of Architecture at Valparaíso stood out for its capacity to turn class exercises into real-life actions of a poetic nature. The Politecnico di Milano excelled at using incipient computers to envision new methods for urban analysis. The architecture schools at Columbia and Yale became loci for the emergence of a strong political activism. In the context of an international group of prominent schools hosting

1. Raimund Abraham quoted from an unpublished and unedited interview recorded April 20, 1993. Courtesy of The Irwin S. Chanin School of Architecture Archive of The Cooper Union.

such significant experiments, Cooper Union singled itself out by focusing strictly on the basis of architectural design.

Here I will be examining the salient elements of Cooper's educational project in order to make sense of its pedagogical methods vis-à-vis the singularity of its design production. The examination will concentrate on the time frame covered by the two major publications of student work released by Cooper Union to date: *Education of an Architect: A Point of view 1964–1971* and *Education of an Architect 1972–1985*. The former accompanied a 1971 MoMA show of the same name—the first (and, so far, one of only two) devoted entirely to the work of a single architecture school.

Hejduk and Architecture Education

Both publications came out under the aegis of John Hejduk, an alumnus of the school. Hejduk enrolled at Cooper Union in 1947 and studied there as an undergraduate for three years. He then went on to obtain a Bachelor of Architecture from the University of Cincinnati (1950–52) and a Master of Architecture from the Harvard Graduate School of Design (1952–53), where he graduated in the last year of Joseph Hudnut's deanship.

In 1954, Hejduk spent some time doing research as a Fulbright scholar at the School of Architecture, University of Rome. That same year his teaching career took off at the University of Texas School of Architecture in Austin. There he came into contact with a number of young instructors who would go on to become influential figures, namely, Colin Rowe, Bernhard Hoesli, Robert Slutzky, and Lee Hirsche, among others. Known as "The Texas Rangers,"[2] this group of educators kept teaching together until 1956, when they were all fired in what Hejduk later judged to be "a blatant suppression of ideas."[3] Hejduk went back to his origins and settled in New York, the city in which he would

2. For a comprehensive study of the pedagogical practices of the Texas Rangers in the 1950s, see Alexander Caragonne, *The Texas Rangers: Notes from an Architectural Underground* (Cambridge, MA: MIT Press, 1995).

3. John Hejduk, in a letter dated December 8, 1986, and addressed to Hal Box, then dean of the School of Architecture at the University of Texas. From Caragonne, *The Texas Rangers*, 412.

spend most of his life. After working for two years at the office of I.M. Pei (1956–58), he taught at Cornell (1958–60) and was hired by Paul Rudolph to serve as a critic in architectural design at Yale (1961–64).[4]

Yale was the last institution at which Hejduk taught before the start of his long-term relationship with Cooper, where he arrived in 1964. Only one year later he succeeded Esmond Shaw as the head of the Department of Architecture, which at that point was still part of The Cooper Union School of Art. The split took place ten years later, in 1975, when The Cooper Union School of Architecture established itself as we know it today and Hejduk was appointed dean. He continued in that position until his passing in 2000.

1964–1971: In the Shadow of the Modern Movement

When Hejduk first arrived at Cooper as an educator in the mid-sixties, the teachings of art and architecture were very much intertwined. The Department of Architecture belonged to the School of Art, both housed in the same building.[5] At the time, both art and architecture students entered what was known as the "foundation program," a sequence of courses to be completed over the first two years of training. It was primarily a Bauhaus type of program, in that it aimed to teach the fundamentals of design for application across different mediums. Students were not asked to emulate Mies van der Rohe or some other master, this being the case, for example, at IIT in Chicago. Rather, it was the pedagogical philosophy embedded in the overall educational strategy that bore the Bauhaus stamp. There was a clear preference for abstract two-dimensional and three-dimensional design problems, black-and-white line drawing, conceptual color studies, and collage techniques (fig. 1.1). Some of these exercises had previously been tested at the University of Texas. Indeed, the Bauhaus imprint can largely be traced back to the Texas Rangers. Slutzky and Hirsche were both painters who had studied under Josef Albers at Yale, with Albers being an artist deeply involved

4. See John Hejduk, *Mask of Medusa: Works, 1947–1983* (New York, NY: Rizzoli, 1985), 458.

5. To this day the schools of art and architecture are housed in the same building, the so-called Foundation Building on Cooper Square, in New York City. The last renovation of the building, by John Hejduk himself, was completed in 1974.

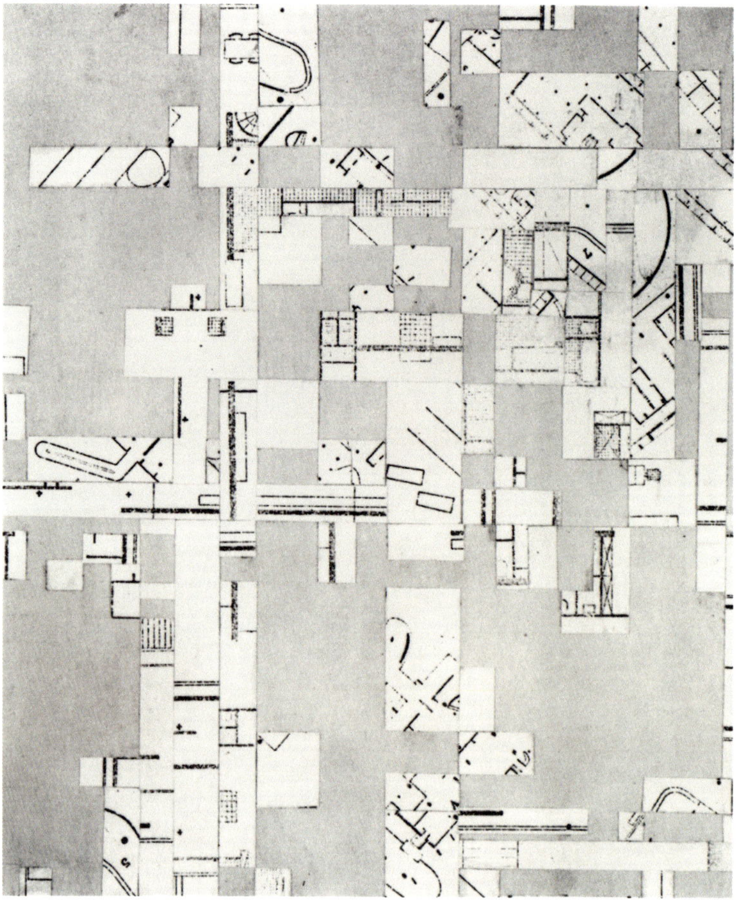

1.1 Daniel Libeskind, *Collage*. Thesis, 1969–70.

with the Bauhaus both as a student and a teacher. Slutzky went on to teach at Cooper.

It was at Texas, too, that the most popular of those design exercises was born: the nine-square grid problem. Conceived by Hejduk along with Slutzky and Hirsche, this exercise targets the grounds of the language of architecture in a radical fashion. What is meant here by "language of architecture" is as follows. On the one hand, there are the units that make up an architectural vocabulary: column, wall, ceiling, floor slab, and in general, all of the elements into which an architectural artifact can be broken down. On the other hand, these basic "bricks"—or "words," if we were to use a linguistic analogy—become a three-dimensional architectonic unity by virtue of the spatial relationships established between them. It is worth quoting Hejduk at length here for his didactic description of those two distinct yet related aspects:

> The problems of point-line-plane-volume, the facts of square-circle-triangle, the mysteries of central-peripheral-frontal-oblique-concavity-convexity, of the right angle, perpendicular, perspective, the comprehension of sphere-cylinder-pyramid, the questions of structure-construction-organization, the questions of scale, position, the interest in post-lintel, wall-slab, vertical-horizontal, the arguments of two-dimensional and three-dimensional space, the extent of a limited field, of an unlimited field, the meaning of plan, of section, of spatial expansion-spatial contraction, spatial compression-spatial tension, the direction of regulating lines, of grids, the meaning of implied extension, the relationships of figure to ground, of number to proportion, of measurement to scale, of symmetry to asymmetry, of diamond to diagonal, the hidden forces, the ideas of configuration, the static with the dynamic—all these begin to take the form of a vocabulary.[6]

In Peter Eisenman's terminology, such internal conditions of the language of architecture must be referred to as *intrinsic*. These are to be distinguished from the *extrinsic* conditions encompassing its *expressive content*, i.e., its capacity to appeal to the senses on the one hand and to generate meaning

6. Hejduk, in a philosophical statement written for *Who's Who in American Architecture* in 1988, quoted in Caragonne, *The Texas Rangers*, 373.

on the other.[7] The nine-square grid problem was not about addressing the extrinsic conditions; the exercise is all about *syntax*, not *semantics*. Students were asked to "build a model at ¼" = 1' -0 scale" of a sketch simply depicting a 16' by 16' grid of columns, and "to begin to study spatial relationships within that grid."[8] They were then required to "draw their schemes in plan and in axonometric, and search out the three-dimensional implications in the model (fig. 1.2)."[9]

Along with the different modalities of drawing exercises and the abstract design techniques (such as the nine-square grid problem), the third key component of Cooper's teaching philosophy put in practice during the first period of Hejduk's leadership was the analytical approach to the study of historical buildings. Rather than the usual emphasis on the examination of specific stylistic formats, each student was asked to draw, make models of, dissect, and analyze the structural and organizational features of either a representative work by a twentieth-century master or a historical building of significance. Le Corbusier's church in Firminy, for instance, was one such typical case study subjected to analysis.

A pedagogy of architecture delineated through these three practices seeks to set aside, if not reject, the notion of "style," something on which Hejduk insisted repeatedly throughout his career.[10] To take the nine-square grid problem, this is an exercise that highlights the different ways in which a diverse group of students handles a neutral tectonic landscape. Far from imposing any stylistic bias *a priori*, it has the capacity to favor freedom of expression and consequently to allow the individual hand emerge. However, the lack of references one would expect to find in the projects resulting from such generic methodologies was not quite achieved during the first period of Hejduk's leadership at Cooper. Indeed, the marked influence of the International Style

7. See Peter Eisenman, *Eisenman Inside Out: Selected Writings, 1963–1988*, Theoretical perspectives in architectural history and criticism (New Haven: Yale University Press, 2004), 122.

8. Hejduk, *Mask of Medusa*, 37.

9. Cooper Union for the Advancement of Science and Art and The Museum of Modern Art, *Education of an Architect: A Point of View 1964–1971* (New York, NY: 1971), 7.

10. See, for example, Hejduk, *Mask of Medusa*, 35, 71.

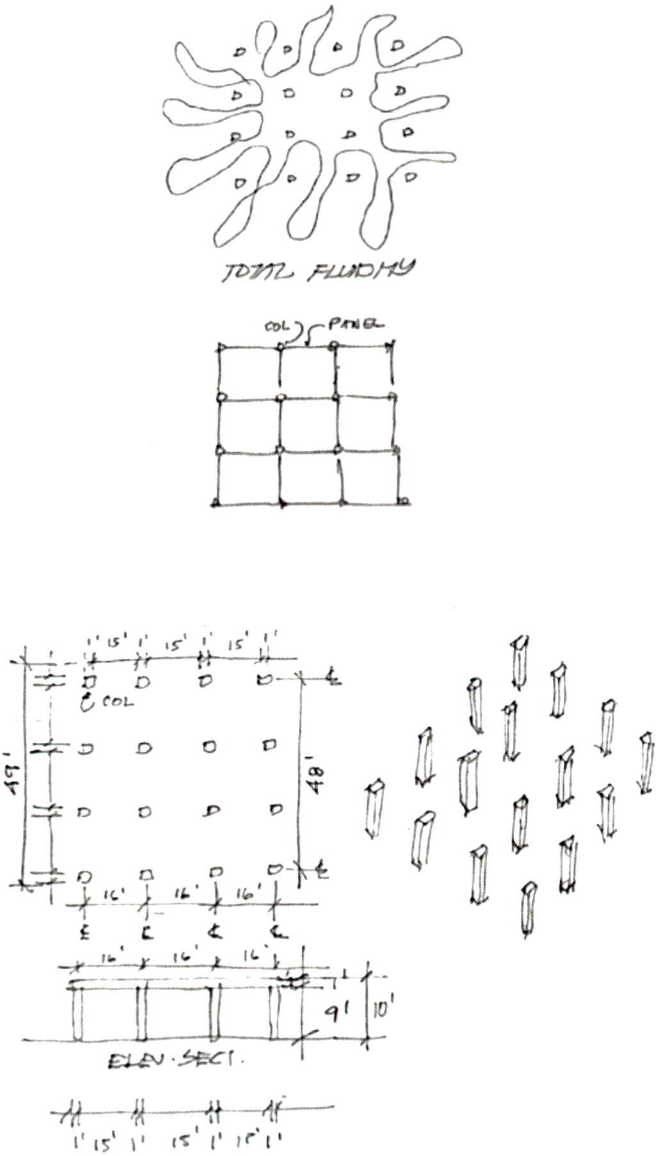

1.2 Initial instructions for the nine-square grid exercise.

in general—and Le Corbusier in particular—is clearly apparent across the design work delivered by the students at the time.

There are at least two reasons for this discrepancy between expectations and results. Firstly, the faculty members teaching at Cooper during Hejduk's early years—educators who, for the most part, he had inherited from the former dean Esmond Shaw—were still very much focused on questions concerning the modernist expressive format that they were trying to advance on the basis of the experiments of Mies and Le Corbusier.[11] Additionally, Slutzky must have further contributed to perpetuating the modernist bent within the school—some commentators judged him to be "parochial about the Modern Movement,"[12] a painter overly concerned with the form-making processes characteristic of modern architecture. Secondly, there is the influence of the work that Hejduk himself was producing at the time. From the mid–1950s through the mid–1970s, the American architect developed a series of houses—Texas, Diamond, etc.—whose design vocabulary was deeply indebted to the great masters of modern architecture. Whether willingly or unwillingly, it seems very likely that this bias came to affect the designs of many of his students at Cooper.

November 13, 1971 – January 10, 1972: The MoMA Show

On November 12 and November 13, 1971, a major conference on architectural pedagogy was held at the Museum of Modern Art in New York City. Under the title "Architectural Education USA. Issues, ideas, and people; a conference to explore current alternatives," panelists included many of the prominent figures active in the US at the time in the emergent field of history and theory: Emilio Ambasz, Stanford Anderson, George Baird, Jonathan Barnett, Peter Eisenman, Kenneth Frampton, Herbert Gans, Robert Gutman, Lionel March, Martin Pawley, Horst Rittel, Colin Rowe, Joseph Rykwert, Denise Scott Brown, Matthias Ungers, and Anthony Vidler.

11. Some of these faculty members included architects Richard Meier, Charles Gwathmey, and his first partner, Richard Henderson, among others.

12. Professor Diane Lewis, interview with the author, December 21, 2010.

Coinciding with the celebration of the event, Arthur Drexler, then curator and director of the Department of Architecture and Design at MoMA, asked John Hejduk to put together an exhibition of student work.[13] Upon the closing of the conference, the show formally opened on the basement level and remained on display through January 10, 1972 (fig. 1.3). Not only was it the first time ever that student work from a single architecture institution was presented at MoMA, but it was also work produced in a relatively small department within a larger school. Hejduk took full advantage of this unprecedented opportunity to showcase the idiosyncratic character of Cooper's architectural pedagogy to a large audience. He turned the exhibit into an educational manifesto, as implicit in the title *Education of an Architect: A Point of View*. A catalogue under the same title—whose uncredited editor was a professor at the school by the name of Roger Canon—was published as a companion to the exhibition and was envisioned as the first installment in a series of books recording bodies of student production, which Cooper set out to release every few years.[14]

Presenting projects from 1964 to 1971, the show illustrated the various design problems and drawing exercises conceived to train students in the fundamentals of the language of architecture. Despite the great significance attributed to the exhibition, especially within academic circles, it was not, however, without criticism. Some saw a kind of "aesthetics" in the students' projects, rather than work with pure syntax that was promoted from within the school as a means towards architectonic innovation.[15]

13. The extent to which John Entenza played a role in Drexler's choice of Cooper Union for the exhibition remains to be properly understood. On the one hand, the first volume of *Education of an Architect* was sponsored by the Graham Foundation, whose director at the time was Entenza. No wonder the book was dedicated to him. In Diane Lewis's words, "John Entenza was a big mentor to John Hejduk." On the other hand, Entenza had already been involved in some other MoMA projects through his rather influential editorship of the *Arts and Architecture* magazine.

14. According to Steven Hillyer, director of Cooper's archive for years and a graduate of the school, the book's print run was very limited, with only 300 copies produced at the time of publication.

15. For instance, Diane Lewis labeled Cooper's pedagogy as "elitist, designy, pretentious, artistic, intellectual, abstract, and non-related to building." Professor Diane Lewis, interview with the author, January 24, 2011.

1.3 *Education of An Architect: A Point of View.* An exhibition by The Cooper Union School of Art & Architecture at the Museum of Modern Art, November 13, 1971 – January 10, 1972.

Similar disapproval developed over the course of the following decade, regarding Cooper's teaching methods as being too far removed from the problems of everyday practice and somewhat "dreamy" owing to their emphasis on intellectual experimentation.[16] There was certainly some degree of accuracy in these views. But it is also true that Hejduk always showed a great deal of interest in fabrication, construction, joinery, and other matter-of-fact questions of the sort. This inclination had an impact on both the development of studio projects—many of which stressed the importance of construction detail—and the school's curriculum, which comprised a notable number of technical courses such as dynamics, structure, and building equipment.

1972–1985: Diversification of Views

The second volume of *Education of an Architect* came out in 1988 and covered the period 1972–85.[17] The book showed the constants and variables of Cooper's pedagogical project throughout the second phase of John Hejduk's leadership, during most of which he acted as dean. Among the aspects that remained nearly unaltered was the design curriculum. The first year was devoted entirely to what was known as "architectonics" in Cooper's culture. Architectonics involved the study of the language of architecture in its most basic formulations; considerations concerning the elements of the architectural order; questions of compression, tension, and spatiality; investigations into the possibility of structural innovation; and notably, the realm of *archi-*

16. See, for example, Crosbie, Michael, "Cooper Union: A Haven for Debate," *Architecture* (August 1984): 48.

17. *Education of an Architect I* was produced quite simply, by featuring one drawing per page, most of which had likely been blown up or scaled down from a photocopy. *Education of an Architect II* was meant to adopt a similar format. However, because of the sheer amount of student work to be published in the book, the thickness of the draft soon revealed that it would have been economically unfeasible. It is for this reason that Hejduk suggested a slightly more complex layout, one where more pictures could be displayed on each page. In terms of editorial agenda, what was deliberately different in this second volume was the intention to have most of the faculty write an essay for the book. This makes sense given the increasing importance that the teaching of literature acquired during the second phase of Hejduk's leadership at Cooper. *Education of an Architect III*, intended to record the ten years spanning 1989 to 1999, was almost ready when Hejduk passed away in 2000. It was expected to be published in 2001, but for reasons yet to be explored, Kim Shkapich—the main person responsible for the project—never followed through.

tectural notation, which stimulated reworkings of the relations between plan, section, and elevation as a design (not only representational) strategy. In the second-year, program and site were introduced, though rarely, if ever, in advance of experimentation with spatial articulation. The idea was not to preconceive an image of a certain type—say, a house—so as not to influence, *a priori*, the purely abstract spatial exercise that was to precede the accommodation of function. In the third year, the first semester was devoted to the analysis problem. As explained above, it was about dissecting, modeling, and drawing a historical work of architecture, which was carried out differently by each student depending on the particularities of each case study. In the second term, a large-scale program, such as a hospital, a theater, or a university, was given.

The city was tackled in the fourth year. Rather than the urban planning approach typical of many schools at the time, the students were required to draw and understand the city at an architectural scale, thereby evincing the clear influence of the Italian scene.[18] Lastly, regarding the thesis (fifth) year, some discrepancies emerge, especially as to the influence of Hejduk on its formulation. Some faculty members claimed that "the fifth year was always John's year. It was defined by John's way of looking at architecture."[19] Others described it on the basis of prompting students to propose a project with barely any initial input and to develop it with the utmost freedom. At any rate, one the most unique aspects of Cooper's thesis system is the fact that no written statement could be used when presenting scope, argument, and proposal. Instead, these were to be put forward through a set of drawings, thus underscoring the importance of architectural expression once again.

18. The connections between some of the prominent figures on the Italian architecture scene and Cooper Union during the 1970s deserves much deeper consideration. A few initial considerations relating to this question are as follows. Massimo Scolari and Aldo Rossi occasionally taught at Cooper during that period. In turn, Hejduk was invited to go to ETH in 1974 to develop a project with Rossi. The Italian architect was probably attracted to Hejduk's interest in the tectonic elements of language and the possibility of investing them with memory. In addition, Diane Lewis studied at the American Academy of Rome in 1976, where she got to know Carlo Aymonino, Manfredo Tafuri, and Carlo Scarpa.

19. Raimund Abraham, unpublished and unedited interview recorded April 20, 1993. Courtesy of The Irwin S. Chanin School of Architecture Archive of The Cooper Union.

While the structure of the design curriculum remained a stable component within Cooper's educational framework, major changes began to take place as to the figures who were to put it into practice. Hejduk's image had arguably been reinforced by the success of the MoMA show. Gaining in confidence and becoming more and more settled at Cooper, he initiated a shifting transformation of the faculty which unfolded over the following fifteen years. Most importantly, in 1971 he brought in Austrian architect Raimund Abraham. Abraham had a marked theoretical approach to the question of language—in particular, Wittgensteinian—and more broadly to the nature of architecture as a poetic practice. His arrival induced Hejduk to get into philosophical questions about form and the *address* of the architectural project, while at the same time it inspired him to break free of an obsession with the problems of form-making tied to the vocabulary of the International Style.[20] Aware of the divergences with Slutzky's position—ever restricted to a promotion of modern abstraction—Hejduk enjoyed bringing the painter and Abraham into heated debates about the nature of form and program. The outcome was the beginning of his break with Slutzky: Hejduk realized that the critiques about the MoMA show were not without reason and the school was indeed running the risk of turning the Modern Movement into a sort of doctrine. Years later, he acknowledged as much when explaining his friction with Slutzky:

> I believe in exploration, always, and I don't believe in the codification of dogma. So, my departure from very close friends from that time is the direct result of not buying into a codification. In other words, I objected strenuously to what they were doing later on at Cornell, where they academized Corb. I had a parting of ways with my old, old friend Bob Slutzky, because I refused to continue that direction down at Cooper Union.[21]

While the Cornell influence—which is to say, the Colin Rowe influence—did not make its way into Cooper via an academicization of Le Corbusier, it

20. Lewis remembers Hejduk often quoting Wittgenstein in class during the early seventies: "What can be seen can never be shown." Professor Diane Lewis, interview with the author, December 21, 2010.

21. John Hejduk in an interview with David Thurman, quoted in Caragonne, *The Texas Rangers*, 367.

did through a didactic utilization of the figure-ground problem, as apparent in the exercises given by faculty members such as Todd Williams, Michael Schwarting, and David Elwell. As for Slutzky, he no longer acted as a professor of architecture after 1981, instead continuing to teach in the School of Art, before leaving Cooper Union for good in 1990.

Following his intellectual opening up, Hejduk became enthusiastic about establishing exchanges with other disciplines. Already during his first years at Cooper, the presence of art was very much felt in the school, as suggested above. Drawing on such artists as Picasso, Juan Gris, Léger, Cezanne, and Braque, there was an emphasis on pushing the relationship between certain breakthroughs in modern painting—notably, cubism and the redefinition of spatiality—and the notation of architecture.[22] But it was only after the MoMA show that the range of fields from which to borrow was considerably expanded.[23] This tendency can partly be identified by looking at the newly hired faculty members. To mention a few of the most significant figures, Hejduk brought in John Hawkes, a novelist and playwright; Davis Shapiro, a poet; and Jay Fellows, a literary critic. The majority of these new acquisitions typically taught elective courses, but at times they would also participate in the teaching of design.

Some commentators have gone so far as to claim that Hejduk should be credited with being one of the first deans of an architecture school who regularly recruited poets, writers, and other artists to become part of the design studio faculty.[24] This statement would require further verification, but certainly one

22. For example, this period saw the development of the well-known and controversial Juan Gris problem, which prompted students to "Do a building in the intention of Juan Gris." See *Education of an Architect: A Point of View 1964–1971*, 163.

23. The permission page that opens the second volume of *Education of an Architect* is quite symptomatic of this. It lists the following names: Haakon Shetelig, Alain-Robbe Grillet, Andre Gide, Jorge Luis Borges, Marion Rombauer Becker, Collete, Antonin Artaud, Sergei Eisenstein, Oskar Schlemmer, Laszlo Moholy-Nagy, Farkas Molnar, El Lissitzky, Marcel Proust, Osip Mandelshtam, Thomas Hardy, Krzysztof Penderecki, and Paul Klee. The Irwin S. Chanin School of Architecture of the Cooper Union, *Education of an Architect 1972–1985* (New York, NY: Rizzoli, 1988), 4.

24. See, for example, *Education of an Architect 1972–1985*, 7, and Caragonne, *The Texas Rangers*, 374. The poets Brian Swann and David Shapiro himself were also involved in studio teaching in the early eighties. See John Crosbie, Michael, "Cooper Union: A Haven for Debate," 47.

such occasion was the spring of 1977, when Hawkes and Fellows were joined by poet John Ashbery, filmmaker Robert Freeman, architect and designer Aldo Rossi, and historian Joseph Rykwert to teach the fifth-year studios at the School of Architecture.[25] By the mid-eighties, even medicine started to play a role in Cooper's pedagogy, with the trigger being a lecture given at the School of Architecture in 1983 by Yale surgeon and author Richard Selzer: "It was mind blowing. He talked about cutting into the body and how he can find a space through the sound of the cut. If architects shouldn't know about that, who should?"[26]

Cooper's disciplinary diversification made it possible to establish analogies between a number of creative practices and the language of architecture so as to gain new perspectives on the latter. The thesis projects best exemplify this pedagogical strategy and most accurately demonstrate the degree of intellectual content that was to be embedded in the design work. A number of these stand out from the period 1972–85. Concerning painting, a student took a late medieval picture and used the conceptions of space, time, and scale found in its pictorial qualities as organizational devices for his proposal. Regarding literature, the relationship with architectural language was at times one of symbolism. In a thesis around Jude—the main character in Thomas Hardy's novel *Jude the Obscure*—the various components of the project were interpreted to recreate events as well as personal features of the protagonist in a significant literary piece. Alternatively, there were also attempts at reconstructing the sequential narrative of a book through architectural images, as was the case in an exercise that used *The Odyssey* as an object of study. Hejduk proposed yet another approach that is relevant here. His chart made in reference to the work of Andre Gide and Marcel Proust suggests a series of qualitative analogies between literature and architecture:

25. See Cooper Union for the Advancement of Science and Art, *Solitary Travelers* (New York, NY: Cooper Union School of Architecture, 1979).

26. John Hejduk quoted in Crosbie, Michael, "Cooper Union: A Haven for Debate," 47.

Sparse	**Dense**
Precision of organization	Elaboration of organization
Precision of structure	Elaboration of structure
Pruned form	Filled form
Planar – two-dimensional	Volumetric – three-dimensional
Linear	Planar
Reduction	Increase
Subtraction	Addition
Clarity	Ambiguity
Sharpness	Bluntness
Shortness	Extensiveness
Tension	Compression
Ambiguity	Clarity
Contractions	Contradiction
Frontality	Multifrontality
Expansiveness	Compactness
Straight – Direct	Elliptical – Oblique
GIDE	**PROUST**[27]

27. Hejduk, *Mask of Medusa*, 51.

In terms of film, a challenging design problem arose when students were asked to superimpose the traditional modes of architectural representation—plans, sections, elevations, and model—and subject them to the narrative of a film in order to seek the emergence of new spatial articulations. In relation to music, one type of exercise involved drawing and dissecting a musical instrument, as in a thesis centered around an accordion and an oboe. In other instances, what was at stake was the transformation of musical notation into three-dimensional architectural language through a particular structural analogy. As for medicine, a rather peculiar exercise purported to turn the vocabulary of dentistry into an architectural language, while another set out to establish a relationship of transference between medical imagery and architectural objecthood. Lastly, even sports were addressed. One student developed a thorough study of billiard ball dynamics—ball hitting, trajectories, traces, etc.—with a view to obtaining a series of proto-architectural drawings through an intermediate, markedly pictorial translation (fig. 1.4).

Self-Determinacy, or the Possibility of an *Uncoded* Architectural Expression

In general terms, Cooper's educational project between the mid–1960s and the mid–1980s channeled a rethinking of the inner logics of the language of architecture: of the main architectural elements (e.g., columns, façade, walls, ceilings, floor slabs) and the principles by which those elements are combined into a recognizable architectonic unit through their three-dimensional disposition in space. In other words, the school stimulated a revision of the foundational components of architectural design, as well as the spatial relationships that can be established between them.

In retrospect, however, the MoMA show can be seen to have marked a shift between two clearly distinguishable periods at the school during Hejduk's first twenty-one years of leadership. The exercises pre-MoMA were stylistically neutral enough to facilitate the development of self-determined modes of architectural expression in line with the creative interests of individual students. Yet much of the work presented a strong modernist bent, reflecting the presence of instructors who continued to be attached to the modern

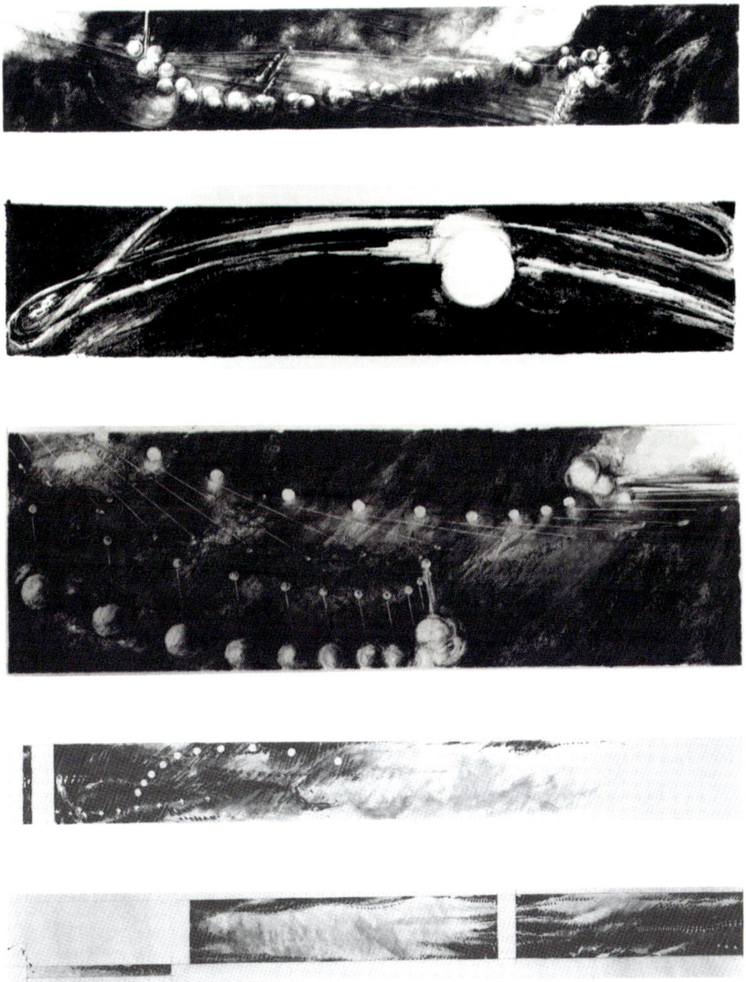

1.4 Jean-Michel Crettaz, *Trajectories and Traces.* Thesis, 1984–85.

architectural vocabulary. In my view, Cooper ended up institutionalizing a style—precisely what one would expect its methodological neutrality to avoid.

After the MoMA show, important changes to the faculty brought about a profound interest in disciplinary expansion. With this came a renewed drive to look at fields other than architecture (and other than modernist painting, which had been the primary source of external inspiration during Hejduk's early years at Cooper). No longer bound by the precepts of the modern movement, the work produced at the school began to display a much more varied array of expressive formats. This diversification demonstrated a methodological aptness to cultivating individuality and difference. Contrary to the somewhat widespread belief that Hejduk used Cooper to disseminate his own idiosyncratic style, explorations of the deepest recesses of the language of architecture, along with intense exposure to procedural schemes characteristic of practices external to architecture (from poetry to medicine), catalyzed the emergence of each student's independent, highly personal voice. In that regard, the central components of the design-related teaching methods put in practice after the MoMA show—some of which arose pre-MoMA and were reframed after the exhibition, while others emerged post-MoMA—proved effective at bracketing out the possibility of engendering a linguistically derivative corpus of architectural work. The Cooper methodology—involving different modes of drawing exercises, abstract design scenarios such as the nine-square grid problem, and an analytical approach to the study of historical buildings—represented an alternative to the reliance on received formats of architectural expression that was commonplace in the 1970s and 1980s at schools such as Princeton, Columbia, and IIT, to name but a few.

Though not always successful in terms of the originality of the final projects, what could be understood as Cooper's quest for linguistic self-determinacy did yield a sizeable body of student work possessing an *uncoded* nature during the 1972–85 period. Instead, exercises where *coded* architectural components were either used to start the drawing process or introduced somewhere along the way, tended to yield mere collages or dislocations of elements, regardless of any interdisciplinary transference. By and large, the more successful instances followed a different logic. First, a set of abstract drawings or models was made that conformed to, or was inspired by, the organizational and expressive principles regulating an extra-disciplinary concept, piece, work, instrument, or modus operandi, which was established as a starting point for an analogy with architectural thinking. These initial sketches, often bearers of remarkable pictorial and material qualities, were then translated into an architectural or proto-architectural ensemble in an unmediated fashion, that is to say, by letting them drive themselves in accordance with their own internal nature, rather than by making use of an intermediary set of recognizable architectural codes (fig. 1.5). The outcome possessed a degree of self-referentiality that lived up to the profound individuality embedded in the very process of its creation.

Architecture production that qualifies as art and also exhibits a marked *uncodedness* liberates itself from received discourse. This exceptionality recalls the framework of Herbert Marcuse's aesthetic theory, in particular his conception of art as *aesthetic form*:

> The radical qualities of art, that is to say, its indictment of the established reality and its invocation of the beautiful image of liberation are grounded precisely in the dimensions where art transcends its social determination and emancipates itself from the given universe of discourse and behavior while preserving its overwhelming presence.[28]

Devoid of clear references, difficult to pin down historically, tending towards the stripping away of recognizable stylistic codes, the projects featuring said *uncodedness* measured up to the potential for singularity that was written into Cooper's teaching methods and testified to their capacity to nurture a certain level of disciplinary instability. By becoming a locus of pedagogical idiosyncrasy outside the prevalent frameworks of academic training, the school established itself as a point of reference for the disruption of the status quo—"a kind of academia outside of academia, a kind of cloister outside of a cloister."[29]

28. Herbert Marcuse, *The Aesthetic Dimension: Toward a Critique of Marxist Aesthetics* (Boston, MA: Beacon Press, 1978), 6.

29. Quote by Peter Eisenman from an unpublished and unedited interview recorded April 20, 1993. Courtesy of The Irwin S. Chanin School of Architecture Archive of The Cooper Union.

1.5 Evan Douglis, *Sound Structures.* Thesis, 1982–83.

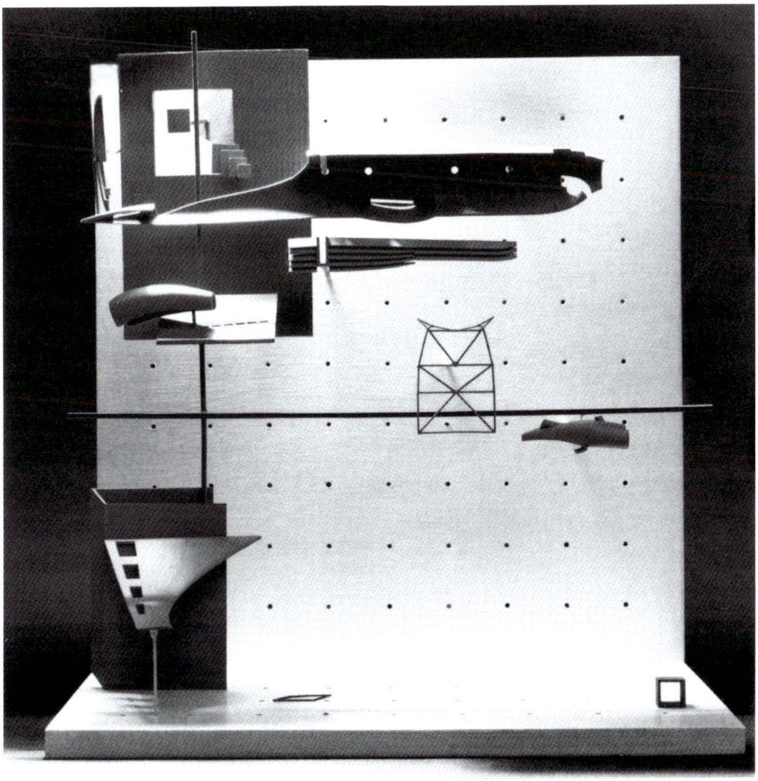

Toward a Critique of "The Organic" in Architectural Thinking[1]

Several historians have pointed out that Aloys Hirt introduced the term "organic" (or "organisch") in architecture in his *Die Baukunst nach den Grundsätzen der Alten* of 1809.[2] Others, such as the Italian architect Alberto Sartoris, have signaled that Fra Carlo Lodoli had already alluded to "architettura organica" one century earlier in *Elementi dell'Architettura Lodoliana, o sia, l'Arte del Fabbricare con Solidità Scientífica e con Eleganza non Capricciosa*.[3] Over and beyond these remote precedents, however, it can be said that the notion of the organic was not formally articulated for architectural purposes until Louis Sullivan's *Kindergarten Chats* of 1901:

1. This essay is based on research carried out at the Columbia University Graduate School of Architecture, Planning, and Preservation. Special thanks to Mary McLeod and Reinhold Martin for their invaluable insights during the construction of the argument presented hereafter.

2. See, for example, Peter Blundell-Jones, *Hugo Häring: the Organic versus the Geometric* (Stuttgart: Ed. Axel Menges, 1999), 83, and Caroline van Eck, *Organicism in Nineteenth Century Architecture: An Inquiry into its Theoretical and Philosophical Background* (Amsterdam: Architectura and Natura Press, 1994), 144.

3. Alberto Sartoris, "Espejuelo para cazar alondras," *Cuadernos de Arquitectura* 17 (1954): 191. *Elementi dell'Architettura Lodoliana, o sia, l'Arte del Fabbricare con Solidità Scientífica e con Eleganza non Capricciosa* is the book of Rodoli's theories compiled by his disciple Andrea Memmo in Rome in 1786. In it, Rodoli alluded to the concept of "organico," in reference to the fact that every form in architecture ought to follow its particular function. See also "Organica, Architettura," in Luigi Grassi and Mario Pepe, *Dizionario della Critica d'Arte* (Turin: UTET, 1978).

> In seeking now a reasonably solid grasp on the value of the word, organic, we should at the beginning fix in mind the values of the correlated words, organism, structure, function, growth, development, form. All these words imply the initiating pressure of a living force and a resultant structure or mechanism whereby such force is made manifest and operative. . . . If the work is to be organic the function of the parts must have the same quality as the function of the whole.[4]

As these and other statements in *Kindergarten Chats* suggest, the American architect's understanding of the organic was based upon an analogy between the methods of nature and those of human creation which, in its structural quality, exceeded sheer mimicry and any other direct formal relationship with the living world.

This conceptualization of the organic echoes a number of epistemologies defining the rapport between art and nature that had been posited much earlier in the field of aesthetics. One only needs to recall here Leon Battista Alberti's notion of *cocinnitas,*[5] the Kantian idea of *system,*[6] or Goethe's theorization of the work of art as something that develops from within, structurally, just

4. Louis Sullivan, *Kindergarten Chats* (Cleveland, Ohio, 1901–1902), 47–48.

5. See Leon Battista Alberti, *On the Art of Building in Ten Books* (Cambridge, Mass.: MIT Press, 1991), 303, trans. from *De Re Aedificatoria* (1443–52) by Joseph Rykwert, Neil Leach, and Robert Tavernor. Alberti's notion of *cocinnitas* referred to a sort of unity and internal coherence that was to be achieved in an architect's work, similar to the way that such attributes are found in the products of nature.

6. In Immanuel Kant's *Critique of Pure Reason* of 1781—cited and translated in Caroline van Eck, *Organicism in Nineteenth Century Architecture: An Inquiry into its Theoretical and Philosophical Background* (Amsterdam: Architectura and Natura Press, 1994), 122—the notion of *system* is described in the following terms: "I consider a system to be the unity of manifold knowledge under one idea. This is the idea formed by the reason of the form of a whole, in so far as such concept determines a priori both the size and the position of the parts in respect to each other. The scientific concept of the reason, therefore, contains the end [Zweck] and the form of the whole, which corresponds to the former. The unity of the end, to which all parts are related . . . makes that every part can be missed if knowledge of the other parts is available, and that no addition, made at random . . . takes place. Thus, the whole is articulated (articulatio), not heaped together (conacervatio); it can grow from within (per intus susceptionen), like the body of an animal, whose growth does not add a limb, but makes every limb stronger and fitter for its purposes without changing the proportions." Kant's thoughts on organic form as being logically driven by an idea that systematically governs the relationships between the parts constituted a crucial precedent for the understanding of organic unity all through the nineteenth century.

as organisms do.[7] The organic, therefore, cannot be taken as an inherently architectural construct. This exteriority renders evident the necessity to examine the philosophical implications of the term "organic" and to critique their intersection with twentieth-century architecture. Only in doing so will it be possible to offer a rigorous assessment of the organic condition as used—or for that matter misused—in discursive and material practices.

The Organic Quality

The adjective "organic" derives directly from "organ," whose etymological roots are the Latin *organa* and the Greek *organon*. These two terms emphasize the idea of instrumentality and come themselves from the Greek *ergon*, meaning "to work." "Organic," then, refers essentially to the qualities of an organ as something that operates in a specific fashion to achieve a particular purpose. Hence the idea of *function* as the driving force behind such instrumentality becoming a fundamental organic precept. The significance of change as something to be accommodated in the development of processes—and ultimately as the goal—is equally crucial for a genuine understanding of the organic: insofar as such processes are substantially determined by time, the contingencies characteristic of any given moment govern the unfolding of realizations, which results in *the dynamic* being another central organic trait.

Other dimensions of the organic concern unity and part-to-whole relationships. The inorganic involves a whole that is understood as the mere sum of the parts, while the organic implies that the way the parts work together in relation to the whole transcends their very sum. Thus, in the organic whole there exists a sort of continuity negotiating the parts, which leads to the achievement of *organic integration*—an idea that prompted the association of the organic with holism,[8] and by extension with a condition of *completeness*

7. See Johann Wolfgang von Goethe, *The Metamorphosis of Plants* (Junction City, OR: Biodynamic Farming and Gardening Association, 2004), trans. taken from the *British Journal of Botany* (1863), revised by Anne E. Marshall and Heinz Grotzke; and *Italian Journey* (New York, NY: Suhrkamp Publishers, 1989), ed. Thomas P. Saine and Jeffrey L. Sammons; trans. Robert R. Heitner.

8. See Jan Christiaan Smuts, *Holism and Evolution* (London: McMillan, 1927).

that became linked to certain theoretical models of social organization in the nineteenth century.[9] Far from merely referring to form or visual appearance, it becomes obvious that the term "organic" relates to actual products and systems, as well as more broadly to processes and principles independently of any one specific branch of knowledge.

When the term "organic" is applied to a particular discipline, *modus operandi*, or material realization, the association of the organic qualifier with a model of nature can be established in a number of different ways, as some commentators have noted.[10] In the first place, the organic *analogy* alludes to a reciprocal correspondence between that which is being categorized as organic and a living model. This is the case, for example, in the parallel between classical art and nature vis-à-vis structural growth, autonomy, and part-to-whole relationships promoted by German Idealist thinking in the late eighteenth and early nineteenth centuries.[11] Secondly, the organic *metaphor* speaks to the character of the association as one following an ideal. It is therefore directional as opposed to reciprocal. Antoni Gaudi's concern for the workings of trees while designing his own structures and algorithmic procedures, striving to simulate natural randomness, constitutes a didactic illustration of organic metaphors. Lastly, a *literal transposition* entails a relationship characterized by visual likeness or mimicry, as in Victor Horta's borrowing of grass, branches, and vascular plants for ornamental motifs.

9. Relevant instances include Émile Durkheim's notion of *organic solidarity* (versus *mechanical solidarity*) and Ferdinand Tönnies' *Gemeinschaft* (versus *Gesellschaft*). See Émile Durkheim, *The Division of Labor in Society*, trans. George Simpson (New York: Macmillan, 1933), especially chapters 2 through 4; and Ferdinand Tönnies, *Community & Society (Gemeinschaft und Gesellschaft)*, trans. and ed. Charles P. Loomis (East Lansing: Michigan State University Press, 1957).

10. Annika Waenerberg, "Organic: A Brief History of the Concept," *Structurist* 47/48 (2007/2008): 41–47.

11. Nineteenth-century organicism, as present in the work and writings of Kant, Goethe, Schlegel, Schinkel and Bötticher, was characterized by a concern for reinterpreting the tradition of classicism through the revealing of new parallels with nature.

Organic vs. Organicist

As the field of natural sciences expanded more and more in the nineteenth century, concerns about instrumentality as defined by the organic began to arise. A problematization of causality—specifically, whether the origin of an action is physical or spiritual—and agency—whether the nature of that which originates the action is either man-made or divine, and either external or internal to a process—prompted ontological distinctions vis-à-vis the question of organic instrumentality. They were rendered differently by three lines of thought: *mechanism*, *vitalism*, and *organicism*. The doctrine of mechanism centered around the so-called "efficient cause," where one step in a process led automatically and predictably to the next, and the agent enabling realizations was found in the laws of physics and chemistry. According to vitalism, the processes of life were steered by a vital principle—one which, as distinct from biochemical reactions, was often associated with the mystical or described in terms of a "Supreme Being." Lastly, organicism defined processes as driven by an agent inherent to the unfolding of a living realization. It alluded to a dynamic system capable of accommodating change, thereby introducing the key idea of evolution.[12]

Two consequences follow on from this schema. Firstly, mechanism and vitalism stressed the relevance of origin, whereas organicism emphasized development. Secondly, it is plain that the term "organic" is broader and has a fairly sophisticated set of implications—as discussed in the previous section—while "organicism" more specifically referred to one of the ways in which an organic realization may unfold.

The articulation of the term "organic" for architectural purposes took place at the turn of the twentieth century, precisely when the doctrine of organicism became the predominant model for explaining the character of natural processes.[13] This historical convergence between an architectural idea and a philosophical outlook may indeed have determined the way in which *the organic quality* has been understood in architecture culture from the early

12. For an extended discussion of these three doctrines see, for example, J. Williams Ruud, *The Organic: Nature, People, Design* (Knoxville, TN: College House Enterprises, 2002), 13–15.

13. See Ruud, *The Organic: Nature, People, Design*, 22.

twentieth century to the present. According to organicism, "truth" is found in living realizations, and as such nature becomes a model. Therefore, the primary **interpretation** of organic processes being of an organicist sort—as opposed to vitalist or mechanicist—explains the propensity of organic thinking in architecture to search for operative analogies between the methods of nature and those of human creation.[14]

It is worth noting the rather different view of the distinction between "organic" and "organicism" held by Bruno Zevi. "Organicism," he maintained in 1950, did not apply to architecture as it implied the idea of a *project*—in the sense of a "dream," a vision, or an enterprise to be accomplished in the future—that had never been formulated. Alternatively, the Italian historian and theorist espoused the use of the term "organic" because he believed that this notion simply described a tendency discernible in architecture at the time.[15]

Sampling "The Organic" in Twentieth-Century Architecture

A survey of organic paradigms in architecture across the twentieth century yields a diverse range of positions, varying according to different social, ideological, and cultural backgrounds. The construction of a historical panorama reveals how different organic references were related to different material realities and visual cultures, as well as how a number of architects and architectural historians deployed organic theories for their own distinctive ends. Let us briefly discuss a few of the most representative cases.

Louis Sullivan's contribution to the organic tradition was introduced above. Upon close inspection, his production manifested a considerable gap between discourse and built work. He theorized some of the central organic features subsequently

14. Strictly speaking, however, one could argue that organicism as an architectural paradigm is an impossibility in principle. As described by this doctrine, the agent of realizations is found within the entity itself that is unfolding. Yet, any work of architecture needs an external agent in order to come into being: the architect. Only the very reduced camp of architectural designers interested in self-generation and auto-poiesis could be rightly considered within the ambit of organicism. These practices look at processes where architecture makes use of living substances in order to generate itself.

15. Bruno Zevi, *Towards an Organic Architecture* (London: Faber and Faber, 1950), 10.

taken up by other organic architects and authors. They included the integral part-to-whole relationships, some vague references to growth, and above all the correlation between form and function that became his well-known slogan. Yet in his designs, Sullivan's organic approach was ultimately grounded in a marked symbolism with ornamental purposes, as duly illustrated by the Transportation Building and the Guaranty Building, both completed in 1894.

Sullivan's disciple Frank Lloyd Wright has long been considered the organic architect *par excellence*. A deep concern for the environmental factors present, for example, in his Usonian Houses; a close rapport between building and site; the introduction of biological metaphors, as in the St. Mark Tower; a progressive distancing from the constraining box to give way to what he termed "open planning"[16]—all of these represent just a few features in Wright's work that can be referred to as organic.

Across the Atlantic, German architects Hugo Häring and Hans Scharoun were exemples of "the organic functionalist," an idea promoted by architectural historian Adolf Behne in the 1920s. Their main contributions to the organic tradition lay in their emphasis on circulation and flow patterns for the genesis of plans, as well as in the necessity to conceive of function and expression side by side. Scharoun specifically added a heavy reliance on the notion of growth in his use of geometry and an emphatic concern for climatic and acoustic considerations, both in the Philharmonic of 1963 in Berlin and in the German Embassy of 1971 in Brasilia, to mention a couple of examples (fig. 2.1). The term *responsiveness* comes to mind as a way of characterizing Häring and Scharoun's organic approach to client, site, environment, and program.[17]

16. The Wrightian notion of "open-planning" rejected having to respond to a predetermined prototypical shape. The relationships between internal spaces being fluid and variable challenged the traditional idea of "room." As a result of such freedom in the unfolding of the interior, the external volume did not follow a preconceived geometric order. Fallingwater House, for example, was to illustrate this philosophy of design.

17. The term "responsiveness" was used by Peter Blundell-Jones to designate the attention to specific details of reality that organic thinking commonly exhibited, in contradistinction to an obedience to imposed, abstract rules. On this matter, organic processes were open-ended in that they enabled the different components to develop according to the contingencies of a particular scenario. See Peter Blundell-Jones, *Hugo Häring: The Organic versus The Geometric* (Stuttgart: Ed. Axel Menges, 1999), 84–89; and Peter Blundell-Jones, "Organic versus Classic," *Architectural Association Quarterly*, vol. 10, no 1 (1978): 10–20.

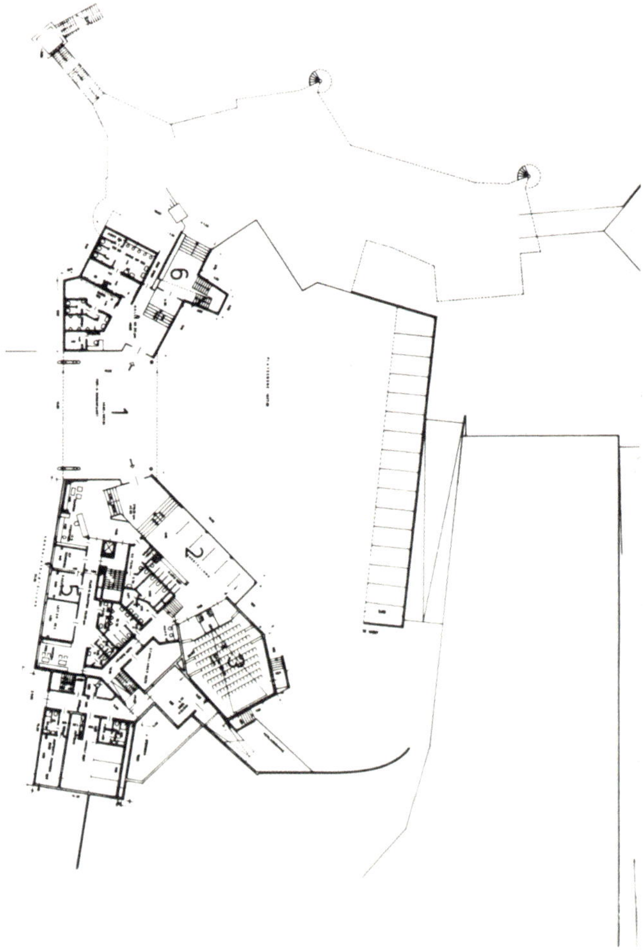

2.1 Hans Scharoun. German Embassy in Brasilia (1964–1971). Ground floor and first floor plans (left and right, respectively).

7
8
9
10
11
12
13
14
15
16
17
18
19
20
N

After WWII, Bruno Zevi rose to prominence as the first author who deliberately revived the organic tradition. He attempted to theorize it as a forgotten branch of the Modern Movement. Beyond figurative and procedural considerations, for him organic architecture was one whose "spatial arrangement of room, house, and city are planned for human happiness, material, psychological, and spiritual."[18] The Italian historian and theorist rejected the idea of imitating nature and the use of terms intended to describe living beings for architectural purposes.[19] Above all, he stood for the organic as a social and psychological project.

Organic agendas influenced by a fascination with the vernacular were perhaps best embodied in the work of Scandinavian architects Alvar Aalto and Jørn Utzon. Aalto's approach was driven by a particular curiosity about architectural materiality and by the integration of standardization and irrationality, otherwise commonly opposing tendencies. In Utzon's case, his *additive architecture* evinced a marked preoccupation with the idea of growth via the fusion of "the geometric" and "the organic,"[20] where the latter was meant to result from the former.[21] In addition, specific works such as the carapace-like Sydney Opera House revealed a parallel interest in symbolism which clearly echoed that of Eero Saarinen in his bird-like TWA Terminal building, one of the milestones in twentieth-century organic architecture.

Another salient organic author was designer, architect, and artist Frederick Kiesler. *Continuity*, in the way that it drove his notion of "endless space," constituted the central aspect of his organic thinking.[22] His rejection of the

18. Zevi, *Towards an Organic Architecture*, 76.

19. Zevi, *Towards an Organic Architecture*, 75. For Caroline van Eck, Zevi's attitude stood in stark opposition to the tradition of organicism in nineteenth-century architecture, since his conceptualization of the organic avoided a connection with nature altogether. See Caroline van Eck, *Organicism in Nineteenth Century Architecture*, 267.

20. I borrow the term "additive architecture" from Phillip Drew. See Phillip Drew, *The Third Generation: The Changing Meaning of Architecture* (New York: Praeger, 1972), 44–46, quoted in Kenneth Frampton, *Studies in Tectonic Culture: The Poetics of Construction in Nineteenth and Twentieth Century Architecture* (Cambridge, Mass.: MIT Press, 1995), 247.

21. See Frampton, *Studies in Tectonic Culture*, 267.

22. Indeed, this idea was for him something of an obsession, as he hinted toward the end of his life: "I shall stick to my travel along my old lifeline to seek continuity." Interview with Thomas H. Creighton, "Kiesler's pursuit of an idea." *Progressive Architecture* (July 1961): 123, quoted

“four-fold division of column, roof, floor, wall”[23] and his Endless House represented the conceptualization and the materialization, respectively, of an idea that has often been credited to architects of the 1990s, namely the spatial dissolution of structural elements.[24] Further, Kiesler advocated for a social project grounded in the possibility of “building adequate to the elasticity of living functions,”[25] an aspiration that “will remould society.”[26] His background in the intellectual circles of Social Democratic Red Vienna laid the foundations for his later promotion of a rationally based system of social relationships, in which the pursuit of freedom and happiness very much recalls Zevi’s ideal.

Buckminster Fuller emerges as another central author who made significant use of organic precepts throughout his *oeuvre*. As K. Michael Hays noted, “[f]or Fuller everything that exists is a modulation of something else, an articulation of one substance.”[27] Fuller’s deliberate stress on the creativity of the individual, his will to find the source of innovations and discoveries in nature,[28] his ecological concerns, and his quest for environmental performance might be cited as some of the organic principles driving his work. His projects involving structural growth—from which Louis Kahn, among others, later drew inspiration—probably became his main contribution to twentieth-century organic discourse.

in Dieter Bogner, “The Endless House,” *Friedrick Kiesler 1890–1965*, ed. by Yehuda Safran (London: Architectural Association, 1989), 42.

23. Frederick Kiesler, “Notes on Architecture, The Space House,” *Hound and Horn* 6, no. 3 (1934): 282–97, quoted in Bogner, “The Endless House,” 46.

24. Examples include FOA’s Yokohama Terminal—in terms of the disappearance of recognizable structural elements—and Toyo Ito’s Sendai Mediatheque—with regard to the dissolution of vertical supports.

25. Frederick Kiesler, *Die Stadt in der Luft* (Paris, 1925), quoted in Bogner, “The Endless House,” 42.

26. Ibid.

27. K. Michael Hays, “Fuller Geological Engagement with Architecture,” in K. Michael Hays and Dana Miller (eds.), *Buckminster Fuller: Starting with the Universe* (New York: Whitney Museum of American Art, in association with Yale University Press, 2008), 9.

28. “It’s the way nature behaves, so we both discovered nature. It isn’t something you invent. You discover it,” from Dorothy Harley Eber, “Prologue: An Interview with Buckminster Fuller,” in *Genius at Work: Images of Alexander Graham Bell* (New York: Viking Press, 1982), 11, quoted in Dana Miller, “Thought Patterns: Buckminster Fuller the Scientist-Artist,” *Buckminster Fuller: Starting with the Universe*, 24.

Louis Kahn himself, Fumihiko Maki, and Alison and Peter Smithson are also worth mentioning as they built on Fuller's interest in growth as an organic attribute, albeit each with different applications. Kahn's collaboration with Anne Tyng engendered a preoccupation with topological arrangements that revolved around an understanding of structural form as a flexible disposition. In his quest for a combination of monumentality and attention to the human scale, the relationships between spaces and their connection—or disconnection—being dependent upon distance were privileged over the particular shape of the building. In other words, the local behavior between units determined the constitution of the whole, this not being shaped *a priori*. This design ideology can be found in projects such as the City Tower (1952–1957) (fig. 2.2), the Adath Jesurum Synagogue (1954), and the Adler House (1954). On the other hand, both the Smithsons's ideas on "growth and change" and Maki's "investigations in collective form" sought to introduce the notion of time into urban growth as an essential factor (fig. 2.3). Described by Maki as "dynamic equilibrium,"[29] the idea was for the individual components—buildings, roads, services, etc.—to allow for the integrity of the whole, while remaining capable of developing freely so as to accommodate unpredictable changes over time.[30]

An emphasis on scenography and representation fostered by a number of post-modernist agendas and the subsequent deconstructivist pursuit of fragmentation kept organic discourses somewhat dormant during the late 1970s and 1980s. Nevertheless, the emergence of computer-aided design in the 1990s led to a renewed interest in integration, totalities, and dynamics. It was in this regard that the figure of Gregg Lynn stood out conspicuously with his early attempts at theorizing the phenomenon of digital architecture. In his 1999 manifesto, *Animate Form,* Lynn championed an architectural thinking based upon the negotiation of flow and time. For him form was conceived dynamically, its generation triggered by natural forces interacting in virtual space. His theoretical proposition, very much in tune with attributes and precepts relating to the organic, still remains radically topical over twenty years after its formulation: "[t]he challenge for contemporary architectural theory

29. See Fumihiko Maki, *Nurturing Dreams: Collected Essays on Architecture and the City*, ed. Mark Mulligan (Cambridge, Mass.: MIT Press, 2008), 44.

30. See Alison Smithson, *The Charged Void: Urbanism* (New York, N.Y: Monacelli Press, 2005), 56.

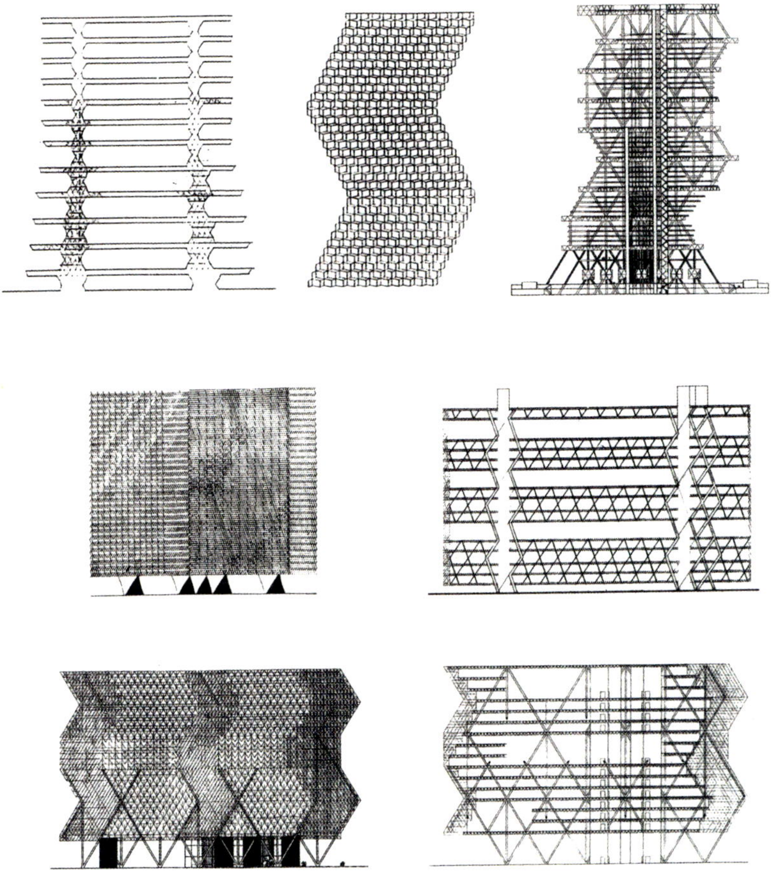

2.2 Louis I. Kahn and Anne Tyng. Above: hypothesis of vertical growth of the geometric system used for the Yale Art Gallery, now applied to the City Tower project. The drawings show the three stages of the tower's design process (1952–1957). Below: initial proposals for the City Tower project (1952–1953).

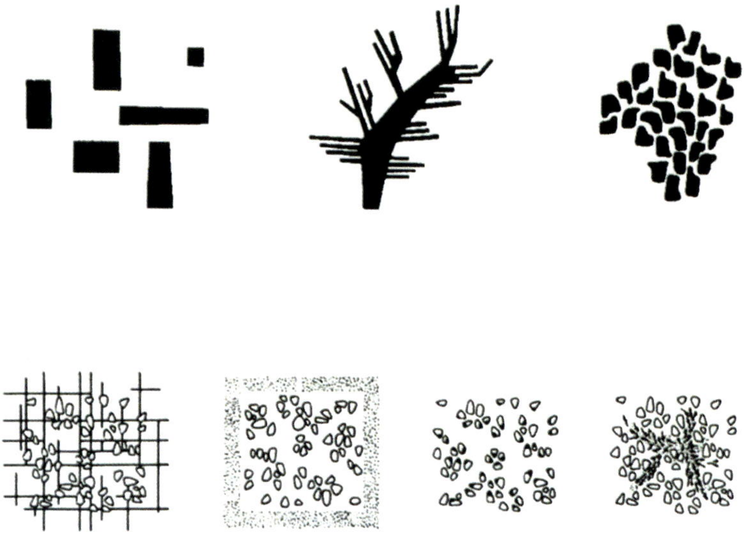

2.3 Fumihiko Maki. Above: Three approaches to collective form (from left to right): compositional form, megaform, and group form. Below: Diagrams representing linkage operations (from left to right): mediation, definition, repetition, and making a sequential path.

and design is to try to understand the appearance of these tools in a more sophisticated way than as simply a new set of shapes."[31]

Toward a Critique of "The Organic" in Architectural Thinking

Tracing the intellectual origins of the organic quality and scrutinizing its philosophical underpinnings problematizes the way in which organic architecture has characterized itself, leading to an important question, namely, to what extent has the appropriation of the term "organic" been too limited or too partial? Indeed, one could claim that certain assumptions and reductionisms may have often been conducive to facile clichés, formal analogies, and biological metaphors. The implications of the organic paradigm, as shown earlier, come before *shape*, since they largely involve procedural strategies, relational properties, and constitutive logics.

I have discussed here a number of architects and authors who have usually been regarded as organic, as well as a few others not so readily associated with that label. However, this attempt to expand the understanding of the organic in architecture ought to be taken much further. In addition to the cases mentioned above, what about architects and thinkers not typically considered organic, whose production might also reveal implicit organic principles? To what extent, for example, might Mies van der Rohe's architectural thinking be partly seen as organic? What features of the philosophical notion of the organic have remained unexplored or overlooked? What architectural attributes would have resulted had these other shades of the term "organic" been taken into consideration? These questions open up a different debate regarding the question of the organic in architecture, one yet to be properly held. An important scholarly contribution still remains to be made by developing a theory of the organic in twentieth-century architecture from a theoretical and philosophical standpoint. A critical approach to the *oeuvre* of some of the central twentieth-century architects through the lens of organic principles would enable both a unique account of their contribution and a parallel reading of the major architecture movements.

31. Greg Lynn, *Animate form* (New York: Princeton Architectural Press,1999), 17.

The Building's Discursive Building[1]

Over the last few decades, architectural history and theory have done a remarkable and necessary job of expanding their limits and audiences. The flip side of this expansion, however, has been a marked displacement of the building as an object of discursive knowledge,[2] ultimately leading to a certain neglect of *architectural thinking* proper. At the other end of the spectrum, discussions centered firmly around design processes and outcomes have often proved self-referential (e.g., those around "autonomy") or restricted

1. "The Building" (www.thebuilding.info) was a six-year project led by José Aragüez between 2014 and 2019. It is widely regarded in international circles as one of the most significant contributions to architectural discourse in the 2010s. The project was launched through two symposia held at the Architectural Association (London) and Columbia University (New York) in 2014, and a theory seminar at Cornell University in the fall of 2015. In late 2014 "The Building" became a book project, the outcome of which was published by Lars Müller in November 2016. More than 400 people are estimated to have directly participated in or helped with the project, which overall generated an unprecedented total of twenty-three events—conferences, lectures, and panel discussions—across Europe and the US. A vast majority of the key figures on the discursive scene worldwide contributed to "The Building." The essay presented here is an adaptation of the introduction to the book of *The Building*.

2. Throughout this essay, the term *discursive* is used in its classical sense, i.e., alluding to the kind of knowledge that involves premises, narratives, judgments, inferences, concepts, ideas, conclusions, etc., as channeled through thought and expressed through language. In the context of architecture, it is important to distinguish *discursive* from *representational* knowledge, which instead proceeds through images, drawings, models, etc., and is associated with design and related practices, such as graphic analysis. The target of this project is the former, not the latter (also sometimes referred to as *non-discursive*). Though different in principle, these types of knowledge can be related. Indeed, it is relatively commonplace to use representational knowledge as a vehicle to produce discursive knowledge.

to the spheres of practice and studio teaching alone. The project laid out in this essay constructs a bridge between these two tendencies by mobilizing a topic—"the building"—that typically belongs in the latter, while seeking the expansion of the former. If the dominant approach driving architectural history and theory today concerns identifying novel subject matter, here the challenge instead involves taking up one of the discipline's oldest themes and reconfiguring it through the intellectual tools now at our disposal. This project therefore invokes the building in order to galvanize architectural thinking's distinct capacity to engender far-reaching concepts, and more generally, discourse.

——

> There is very little reference to buildings and surprisingly little to a building, but there is a powerful ghostly presence of *the* building.[3]

Regardless of how many other agents, layers of discourse, and multiple aspects we bring into focus, the building remains the necessary condition for a contribution to knowledge in architecture. It is in this sense that the building defines its basis: algae may be relevant to architecture, but only if they are nested on a façade that happens to be the component of a building; an investor may be pertinent to the field, but only if he is involved in the development of a series of buildings; bills and rental agreements may be germane to architecture, but only inasmuch as they relate to buildings; drawings are an essential part of architectural discussions, but only because they constitute the medium through which to generate and represent an external reality (the building); the study of a certain community may fall within architectural discourse, but only insofar as it lives or otherwise interacts with a building of some kind; and so on. The same necessity is not true of those agents, layers of discourse, and other aspects when considered by themselves—again, as long as what is at stake is architecture, and not biology, sociology, politics, economics, media studies, etc. The necessary condition would be other if the target were urbanism; product, furniture, or exhibition design; etc. This distinction between fields—either within or beyond design—is a prerequisite for esta-

3. My emphasis. See Mark Cousins, "Afterword," in José Aragüez, ed., *The Building* (Zürich, Switzerland: Lars Müller Publishers, 2016), 398.

blishing any rapport between them, since relationships will only be possible if the *relata* are different to begin with. Moreover, interactions and overlaps can only be productive if those differences are comprehensively accounted for; otherwise, it will not be possible to reach an accurate understanding of such interdisciplinary processes and their results.

> How strange it is to hold a series of conferences, and to work with such fervor to produce an ambitious book . . . on buildings. In architecture. We do not think of folks in biology saying, "Whoa, let's do a book on living organisms," or journalists getting together for a conference about whether or not we should have newspapers. What odd turn of events brought us to this moment? What disciplinary weirdness must have transpired to force the center to snap back into our attention, and require (of all things) weighty discussion?[4]

By "center," Dora Epstein Jones seems to refer precisely to that necessary condition constituted by the building, around which everything else gravitates—in other words, to the fact that, within architecture, the building has *ontological primacy.* So, as she asks, "what odd turn of events brought us to this moment?"

Spurred by an unprecedented awareness of theory's role in constructing architecture's disciplinary culture, the production of knowledge—mainly in the most advanced segment of architecture,[5] but also elsewhere—started to undergo a major transformation during the 1960s. This transformation occurred in an opening up to various other systems of thought (such as semiotics, psychoanalysis, Marxism, and structuralism) and a consequent rewriting of some of those systems' key concepts (e.g., "reification," "signifier/signified," "deconstruction," "rhizome," and "ideology") into architecture's idiolect.[6]

4. Dora Epstein Jones, in an early version of her contribution to *The Building*.

5. This segment consists of the scene around a largely elite university crowd in the US and their European interlocutors. The following history of the shift from the 1960s forward is undeniably tied to this population.

6. For an extended discussion of this discursive phenomenon, see Kate Nesbitt, ed., *Theorizing a New Agenda for Architecture: An Anthology of Architectural Theory 1965–1995* (New York: Princeton Architectural Press, 1996), 12–17, and K. Michael Hays, "Introduction," in *Architecture Theory since 1968* (Cambridge: The MIT Press, 1998), x–xv.

Architectural history and theory established relationships with non-disciplinary structures and social realms (philosophy, linguistics, psychology, anthropology, etc.) through the use of those *mediatory concepts.* Importing thus became a pattern, one still dominant today. The rapport of transference is set between two codes from two different fields in such a way that one of them—architecture—borrows from the other. This unidirectionality, fundamentally at odds with related discursive operations such as Fredric Jameson's *transcoding*,[7] is called into question here.

A tendency to apply external paradigms inevitably recalls the view generally held in the domain of theory—now more generally construed—about the generation following that of the so-called "age of high theory." Unable to produce a comparable body of work, the group of authors that came to prominence around the early to mid-1990s displayed an inclination to reutilize the ideas of the preceding generation—of figures like Lacan, Lévi-Strauss, Derrida, Said, Kristeva, Foucault, and Jameson himself:

> Those who can, think up feminism or structuralism; those who can't, apply such insights to *Moby-Dick* or *The Cat in the Hat.*[8]

To what extent has architecture been able to think up systems of thought specific to itself? In fact, to what extent has architecture been able to think up systems of thought at all? Out of an investigation into the linguistic sign—an object of study pertaining specifically to linguistics—arose structuralism, a broader epistemological apparatus that became relevant across the humanities and social sciences. Other examples include Freudian psychoanalysis,

7. *Transcoding* involves the assessment of the conceptual possibilities—that is, what is sayable and thinkable—of two different codes in comparison with one another, where code stands for a language, an idiolect, or a particular discourse. The ultimate goal of this operation would be to produce a new code, one that "in no way can be considered a synthesis between the previous pair," being rather "a question of linking two sets of terms in such a way that each can express and indeed interpret the other." Jameson clarified that there would be no a priori hierarchy between the two sets of terms or codes, nor an assimilation or borrowing moment that imbalances the equation. Rather, it would be a mutual re-interpretation and re-structuration. The existence of a distinguishable move within architecture history and theory, in which one direction prevails over the other, does not fit with the operational logic of transcoding. See Fredric Jameson, *Postmodernism, Or, The Cultural Logic of Late Capitalism* (Durham: Duke University Press, 1991), 394–95.

8. Terry Eagleton, *After Theory* (London: Allen Lane, 2003), 2.

Frankfurt School dialectics, and deconstruction. What architectural equivalents of these systems of thought are capable of exerting a major influence beyond their original disciplinary boundaries?

In parallel to the dynamic outlined above, and especially since the mid-1970s,[9] the status of the building as an object of discursive knowledge grew more and more unstable as it appeared in more and more guises—whether as the hypostatization of power structures, a facilitator of participatory processes, the locus of phenomenological content, a vehicle to reflect upon unmediated practices, a catalyst for investigating the psychology of perception, or a construct amenable to mirroring processes in the natural world, to name a few examples. While this diversification is an index for the increasing sophistication of architecture as a field, the building itself emerges as a medium through which to tap into another domain—if not as altogether absent—more often than as a realm of research in its own right. For a few decades now, therefore, the building has primarily been a means rather than an end in architectural history and theory.

By virtue of originating in another sphere of knowledge, those mediatory concepts that were pivotal to the theoretical turn carried with them a host of non-architectural associations. Inevitably, in demanding a working-through of their original regime of signification so they could be grasped from within architecture, the internalization of those concepts prompted an attention shift toward the fields from which they were imported. This realignment in focus contributed significantly to the displacement of the building as an object of discursive knowledge, which in turn caused a certain estrangement of the discipline, given the fundamental link between building and architecture. It can therefore be argued that the two dynamics outlined above converge into one, which we can refer to as *estranging internalization*. This logic has to a large degree defined the ways that architectural history and theory have engaged with other fields during nearly the last six decades.

The project articulated here aspires to serve as an inflection point within that trend by suggesting that discussions taking the building as their central

9. Not coincidentally, this is right around the time that Manfredo Tafuri's work started to influence international audiences.

object of critical analysis can substantially extend the bounds of possibility for the production of discursive knowledge in architecture—"the building" constituting the architectural object of knowledge *par excellence*. The project's agenda is twofold: first, to discuss what it means for a building to embody a historically significant contribution in terms of a particular design aspect or concept relevant to the reading of buildings in general; and second, to venture ways in which buildings themselves can induce theoretical frameworks whose impact might extend beyond architecture into other domains of knowledge and practice.

In tackling the building itself as a realm of research in history and theory, this project sets out to probe *architectural thinking* as a central discursive category in its own right. Writings about buildings in the American tradition are frequently identified with the formalist genealogy of Rudolf Wittkower, Colin Rowe, and Peter Eisenman. Some readers versed in that lineage might therefore view this project as a return to "form." However, a building is not "form." Or rather, it is not only form. At the very least, it is a combination of "form" and "program"—one that yields a recognizable unity, the dismemberment of which can only be the effect of rhetoric.

More comprehensively, a building is a material construct made up of a number of elements—and the relations between them—that houses a set of human activities through a permeable sequence of spaces. Granted, that program may vary over time, and the same form might be able to accommodate several different programs based on changing demands and obsolescence. Yet, "program" here does not designate a particular programmatic package—say, a "library," a "house," or a "museum." Instead, it points to the fact that, for a three-dimensional form to be "architectural," it ought to have the capacity to readily house a set of human activities. This is by no means the case for every conceivable three-dimensional form, which is why one cannot say that a building is only form. For example, most of the forms generated through algorithmic and parametric design are so complex, dense, and entangled—featuring proportional relations of such a disjunctive nature—that they cannot house a set of human activities in any realistic sense. Hence they fall within the domain of computer graphics, sculpture, or morphology, rather than architecture. Therefore, if there is at once a loose fit between form and program and a necessity for the former to be able to incorporate the latter, then we may contend that a building is a three-dimensional form whose defining attribute is that of being *always already* inflected with a programmatic potential. Central to its nature is also the spatial organization articulated within its boundaries, as well as the design processes—like construction, typological operations, and contextual conjectures—that give rise to it.

Architectural thinking is understood here as the repository of discursive knowledge produced through the analysis, discussion, and conceptualization of aspects of those two inextricably related regimes: that of *the building*, and that of *the design process* (which, as a subset of architectural thinking, we might refer to as *architectural design thinking*). It thus becomes clear that a critical attention to building is not to be equated with "formalism" or an aesthetic focus. Architectural thinking is a distinct domain of knowledge whose attributes reach well beyond form and aesthetics—many of them relatable to ontology, technology, and several modes of logic and phenomenology. It distinguishes itself from *urban thinking* in that its primary epistemological object is the building, and not the city.

One other important distinction to make is between *autonomy* and *specificity*, two terms that are often conflated. As is well known, the former has come to be understood principally through the projects that Peter Eisenman and Aldo Rossi developed between the mid-1960s and the late 1970s. Eisenman's undertaking consisted in recasting architectural language as an autonomous system, one where "meaning" became restricted to the intrinsic, syntactic relationships governing its constituents—i.e., to form itself. In other words, he sought to remove all external meaning from the piece of architecture in order to make its components refer only to themselves, thereby recalling early twentieth-century theories of non-objective art.[10] In the words of K. Michael Hays:

> Eisenman saw modernist forms not as simple derivatives of functional needs, but as delineations of the immanent, self-referential properties of architecture itself, as searches for objective knowledge that lies outside both the architectural agent's intentions and the

10. Wassily Kandinsky, for instance, comes to mind. For a deeper insight into Eisenman's early theories, see Peter Eisenman, *Eisenman Inside Out: Selected Writings, 1963–1988* (New Haven: Yale University Press, 2004).

> building's uses, and inside the very material and formal operations of architecture. Such research discovered the new in the given "language" through an articulation and redistribution of its elements.[11]

Rossi, on the other hand, echoing the approach advanced by Durand a century and a half earlier,[12] viewed the city as a source of architectural types that could be detached from their particular time and place, turning it into an abstract, atemporal archive of design elements. Generative and mobile, Rossi's types were decomposed, reconfigured, and redeployed under criteria other than those that determined their original use—by placing them in different contexts, invoking meanings from another epoch, hybridizing them, modifying their fragments and outlines, etc. To cite Anthony Vidler:

> The column, houses, and urban spaces, while linked in an unbreakable chain of continuity, refer only to their own nature as architectural elements. . . . It is clear that the nature referred to in these recent designs is no more nor less than the nature of the city itself, emptied of specific social content from any particular time and allowed to speak of its own formal condition. . . . The need to speak of function, of social mores—of anything, that is, beyond the nature of architectural form itself—is removed.[13]

Although the two kinds of autonomy were clearly dissimilar, they both shared an impetus to reduce architecture to a kind of *itselfness* rooted in the essence of form, and to create a hermetically sealed—"immanent, self-referential"—system from this reduction meant to fall outside of time. In contrast, architectural thinking is not grounded in such itselfness. Firstly, formal reductions of that sort, though a methodological option, are certainly not written into architectural thinking's constitutive purposes—among other reasons because, as discussed above, a building is not just "form" but a more complex construct that is irreducible to one single element or type of ope-

11. K. Michael Hays, "The Oppositions of Autonomy and History," in *Oppositions Reader: Selected Essays 1973–1984*, 1st ed. (New York: Princeton Architectural Press, 1998), x.

12. See Jean-Nicolas-Louis Durand, *Précis of the Lectures on Architecture; With, Graphic Portion of the Lectures on Architecture* (Los Angeles: Getty Research Institute, 2000).

13. Anthony Vidler, "The Third Typology," *Oppositions* 7 (Winter 1977): 293–94.

ration, and that incorporates "program" as a necessary, defining category. A building—and with it architectural design—is therefore social by definition, given the nature of program. Secondly, architectural thinking may or may not search for timelessness or universals. The condition that buildings are on some level bound to their time triggers the pursuit of historically contingent knowledge as a matter of course. Thirdly, architectural thinking is not some closed-off epistemological field, if such a thing were possible. It is instead a permeable one: connected to other fields and to culture at large, it bears a distinct potential to thrust itself outward through those connections—a potential this project attempts to ignite.

All of these distinctions vis-à-vis autonomy noted, architectural thinking is nevertheless a *specific* domain. The processes involved in the design of buildings, as well as the characteristics of the outcome, exhibit a number of particularities that make them fundamentally different from those of a piece of music, a novel, a painting, or a film, notwithstanding the analogies that can be made between those mediums.[14] In short, autonomy is grounded in specificity, but specificity does not imply autonomy.

As a result of the traction generated by the prevalent unidirectionality mentioned earlier and the displacement of the building, architecture has for some decades occupied a blurred, uncertain territory relative to other disciplines in the humanities and social sciences. The tendency to resort to mediatory conceptual frameworks (often in order to validate itself), as well as to avoid deep engagement with its main epistemological object, underpin an ethos for architectural history and theory that may very well be perceived from the outside as somewhat compromised, if not downright apologetic. A significant effect of this ethos has been a decline in the importance of architectural thinking, which began to manifest itself more clearly around the mid-1990s,[15] reaching a critical point today. A dominant strain of current historical and

14. Cf. Diana Agrest, "Design versus Non-Design," *Oppositions* 6 (Fall 1976): 46–49. Note, however, that she refers to the practice of design, not the production of discursive knowledge related to such a practice.

15. Coinciding with the last phase of the journal *Assemblage*, which ended in 2000, and in spite of remarkable efforts like Amanda Reeser Lawrence and Ashley Schafer's journal *PRAXIS*, which started in 1999.

theoretical work simply neglects it as a domain of knowledge in itself, thereby reinforcing the status quo.

Capitalizing on a combination of specificity and non-autonomy, this project proposes an alternative to that state of affairs. It seeks to enable architectural thinking to grow into a potent formation on the general map of the humanities and social sciences, precipitating an upturn in its recent trajectory and catalyzing a further balancing out of the discursive tendencies dominant since the 1960s.[16] Then, the theoretical turn brought about a strong engagement with external disciplines characterized by the importation and illustration of concepts from those disciplines[17]—while the building was used as a vehicle to focus on concerns elsewhere. The engagement advocated here is based upon inverting the former dynamic by inverting the latter. That is to say, it is one in which the building, now turned into the main object of research, is recast to trigger concepts, theoretical frameworks, and, even more ambitiously, systems of thought that can alter fields outside of architecture by becoming meaningfully relevant to them. It thus aims to produce knowledge that is both *architecturally specific* and *generalizable*. In contradistinction to *estranging internalization*, we may refer to this type of engagement as one of *outward projection*.[18]

16. Referring to *architectural design thinking* in particular, Ursprung went so far as to claim that positing it as a realm of scholarship "leads to a vast and still hardly exploited field of inquiry." Philip Ursprung, "What Buildings Know," in José Aragüez, ed., *The Building* (Zürich, Switzerland: Lars Müller Publishers, 2016), 358.

17. Jameson pertinently referred to the difference between this type of externality and the capacity of creative practices to generate their own concepts: "Gilles Deleuze argues that film is a way of thinking, that is, it is a way of doing philosophy, but in purely filmic terms: its concrete philosophizing has nothing to do with the way in which some film or other might illustrate a philosophical concept, and that very precisely because the philosophical concepts of film are filmic concepts, and not ideational or linguistic ones. In a similar move, I would like to argue that architectural space is also a way of thinking and philosophizing, of trying to solve philosophical or cognitive problems." (Jameson, *Postmodernism,* 125).

18. "Projection" is used here in its common meaning of extension, thrust. It is not to be confused with "the projective" in a post-critical sense, which referred to the pragmatism of instrumentalization, the embrace of multiplicity, "the performative," "the diagrammatic," "the atmospheric," and ultimately "the relaxed and easy." See Robert Somol and Sarah Whiting, "Notes around the Doppler Effect and Other Moods of Modernism" (2002), in *Constructing a New Agenda: Architectural Theory 1993-2009*, 1st ed. (New York: Princeton Architectural Press, 2010), 193. In any event, let us recall that the target of the post-critical project was "criticality" in architecture. The project presented here, on the other hand, concerns the nature of the production of knowledge in architectural history and theory.

The project put forward here aims to suggest ways in which this shift is possible: ways in which knowledge grounded in the specificities of architectural thinking can be applicable outside the boundaries of the discipline; ways in which its tendency to import can coexist with its capacity to export. To stay with the same examples, that is exactly what structuralism, Freudian psychoanalysis, Frankfurt School dialectics, and deconstruction were able to accomplish. And that is exactly how architecture could become substantially more germane—even beyond the humanities, in fields like computer science and the culture of Silicon Valley, which already display an inclination to use architectural terms.

By tackling the building in all of its complexity through the repository of intellectual tools available now, this project endeavors to make a contribution to architecture culture that differs from that of a few important authors who have embarked upon related enterprises. Though also invested in writing about buildings by way of architectural thinking, some of those authors devoted themselves mainly to architectural historiography, rather than a larger project encompassing theory in the humanities sense of the term, which includes the possibility of developing full-fledged theoretical systems. Others, writing prior to the 1970s, did not count on the sophisticated intellectual tools that have come to our disposal over the last few decades.[19]

It is also important to note that, while the prospects of cultivating "distinctly and irreducibly *architectural* ideas," of architecture enabling "certain ways of thinking that are irreducible to other modes of thought" and even "producing generalizable concepts" via such types of thinking have been identified earlier,[20] they arose in the context of the production of architectural knowledge being predominantly premised on external paradigms.[21] Strictly speaking, that discursive modality prevents such ideas and ways of thinking from being *irreducibly* architectural—i.e., specific to architecture—since on some level they are *reducible* to the external system of thought and related mediatory concepts that make up their realm of possibility. Seeking to

19. Adolf Behne, Sigfried Giedion, and Bruno Zevi would be among these authors, to cite a few of the best-known names.

20. Hays, *Architecture Theory since 1968*, xi–xii.

21. See ibid., xi, xiii–xv.

expand the milieu of architectural history and theory without largely resorting to mediatory concepts, this project purports to forge original ideas from within the epistemology of architectural thinking while propelling them through the pores that link architecture to other domains of knowledge.[22]

———

The term "the building" here alludes to a general object of discursive knowledge, as opposed to a particular instantiation of *a* building, or the construction process of "building."[23] In exploring ways in which buildings negotiate a set of given conditions by generating and further materializing a number of discursive constructs—for instance, the asymmetry between site and programmatic distribution; the tensions between diagram and built object; contradicting notions of originality and reproduction; the disjointed nature of physical context; the possibilities and limitations of the notion of infinitude; or the existential impact of a particular tectonic atmosphere—the project here proposed intends to show how architectural structures may elicit specific interpretive frameworks. In doing so, the goal is to lay the groundwork for expanding on "the building" as such an object of discursive knowledge and to assemble a platform for the projection of concepts from it. Additiona-

22. The six terms under which the thirty buildings presented in *The Building* were grouped ("elements," "wholes," "content," "context," "referents," and "technology") were selected for being at once directly related to architecture and elemental enough to be central to fields outside it. Thus, they functioned as heuristic devices for exploring the various case studies through a number of questions both intra- and meta-disciplinary. These are as diverse as replication, value, iconography, the urban subject, objecthood, boredom, and the digital, to name a few. As a result, the ideas and reflections in *The Building* proved capable of extending to fields such as cultural and intellectual history, philosophy, literary theory, the city, the arts, and design at large. As Philip Ursprung pointed out in his essay, "What Buildings Know" (Aragüez, *The Building*, 354–65), there is a recognizable relationship between *The Building* and Koolhaas' *Fundamentals*, the theme of the Venice Architecture Biennale that he directed in 2014. Indeed, the chronology indicates the emergence of a *zeitgeisty* sensibility: although the genesis of *The Building* dates back to 2011—much before we knew anything about *Fundamentals*—it was only officially launched in 2014, through two international symposia held at the Architectural Association in London (on June 2, five days before the opening of the Biennale) and Columbia University in New York (on November 15), respectively. The shared sensibility is grounded in the ontological primacy within architecture of the objects of study that both projects invoke. However, the essentialism of Koolhaas' taxonomy, structured around strictly architectural categories, is to be contrasted with the heuristic character of *The Building*'s section titles, afforded by their relevance across various domains of knowledge.

23. Cf. Mark Cousins's, Dora Epstein Jones's, and Michael Young's contributions to *The Building*.

lly, by exploiting the capacity of architectural thinking to spawn conceptual frameworks and systematic thought, in combination with the depth, rigor, and sophistication underpinning the production of scholarship, this project aspires to effectively bridge two fundamental spheres in architecture which today continue to grow further and further apart: that of practice/studio culture and that of history/theory.[24]

24. This scope was further amplified via a deliberate cross-continental approach, and even more through a large group of contributors comprising a striking number of essential voices in the current architectural scene. The range of ages—spanning forty years of views on the question at hand—and the array of different perspectives they represent delivered a set of contents that cut across generations, career stages, and disciplinary boundaries. Authors included deans and academic leaders, as well as architects, historians, theorists, philosophers, and doctoral candidates based at institutions such as Columbia, Princeton, Harvard, and UCLA in the US, and the Bartlett, the Architectural Association, ETH Zürich, and ETSA Madrid in Europe. As a result, *The Building* staged a myriad of interactions between the different perspectives on either side of the Atlantic. In addition, contrary to common practice, *The Building* set out to test the possibility of producing scholarship through brief, synthetic pieces and a deliberate engagement with contemporary material.

Sponge Territory

The Taichung Metropolitan Opera House finally opened in September 2016. A winning competition entry from 2005, designed by Toyo Ito with Cecil Balmond as engineer, Taichung is the first of its kind. There is no precedent for a building like this in the history of architecture other than Ito's own 2004 runner-up submission for the Forum for Music, Dance, and Visual Culture in Ghent, Belgium (fig. 4.1).[1] Both projects proposed a double-curved surface that gives rise to two out-of-phase series of coupled spaces, each of which are vertically and horizontally continuous. While Taichung, which houses three theaters and a shopping mall, is larger than Ghent would have been (one auditorium and a number of rehearsal rooms, foyers, and workshops), they are similar enough in scale that the results lend themselves to valid comparison. Moreover, both are proposals for the heart of the city.[2]

1. Former Archizoom member Andrea Branzi is credited as co-designer for this project, but the extent of his contribution is unclear. Branzi had not pursued anything like Ghent previously in his career, whereas Ito continued to do so in Taichung, which seems to suggest that the spatial arrangement for the building must have come from the latter's office. Furthermore, Ghent may be seen as the culmination of a number of design concerns that Ito had been exploring for about a decade prior to this, as Juan Antonio Cortés convincingly showed. See Juan Antonio Cortés, "Beyond Modernism, Beyond Sendai—Toyo Ito's Search for a New Organic Architecture," *Beyond Modernism: Toyo Ito, 2001–2005, El Croquis* 123 (April 2005): 39–43.

2. Though their immediate contexts differ: Taichung is located in an open redevelopment area, while Ghent sits on a tighter site surrounded by a quarter of the old town and the Muinkschelde canal.

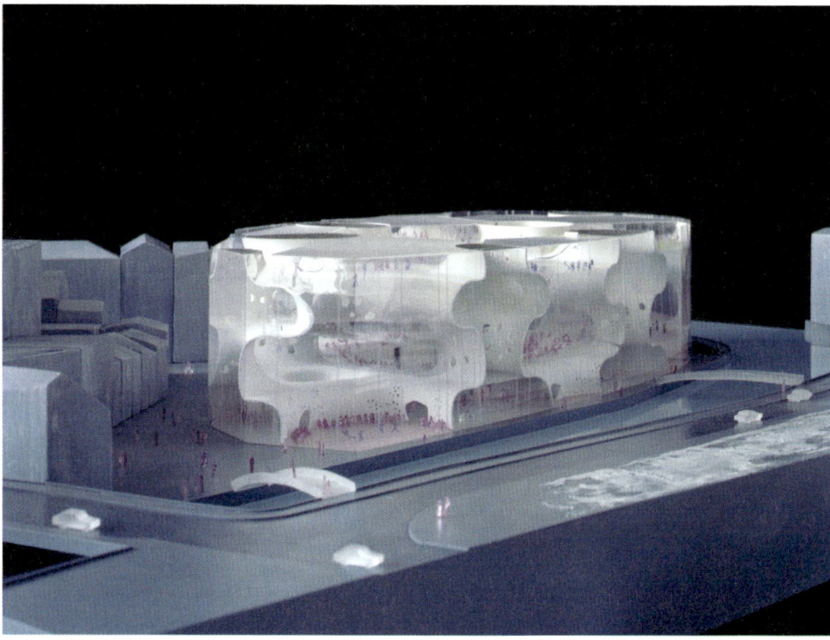

4.1 Toyo Ito + Andrea Branzi. Runner-up competition entry for the Forum for Music, Dance, and Visual Culture in Ghent, Belgium (2004).

Absent in the realm of architectural precedents, the referent for Ito's Taichung is to be found in the world of geometry. Its original kernel is a continuous, unbounded hyperbolic surface of the sort first studied by German mathematician Hermann Schwartz in his *Gesammelte mathematische Abhandlungen* of 1890. Such surfaces take on a sponge-like appearance when extended in space, which led accordingly to the label of "sponge surfaces." Therefore, while newly applied in architecture here, geometers and morphologists have long been acquainted with this type of periodic three-dimensional manifold.

Sponge surfaces possess a number of special characteristics, two of which stand out. First, they are composite patterns of configurational continuity: they combine a compound character—a result of comprising repeating units—with a particular kind of continuity that intricately articulates space by constantly folding upon itself. Second, they subdivide space into two complementary subspaces, which—without ever intersecting—define each other three-dimensionally through sequential interpenetrations (fig. 4.2). These subspaces remain independent across the structure while forming a series of adjacent, interweaving regions throughout (fig. 4.3). A direct connection between the two sets of spaces can only occur if the surface serving as a separating membrane in between is perforated.[3] This condition yields *spatial reciprocity*, whose architectural potential has barely been explored, despite its obvious resonances.

Indeed, architectural design operates frequently on the basis of heuristic binaries—public versus private, open versus compartmentalized, and so on—that might be explored through reciprocal spaces in a particularly productive manner. Taichung's ground floor perfectly exemplifies such reciprocity. A series of closed-off areas, bounded by the surface's vertical segments, contain the back-of-the-house programmatic elements that require partitioning as well as the vertical circulations, while seemingly floating in an undifferentiated continuum of public activities and freely distributed furniture. Serving and served spaces at their purest.

3. Cortés pointed out that each of these two sets of spaces is linked to one side of the same surface. The surface can, in turn, be viewed as resulting from pairing a "form" with its "counter-form." See Cortés, "Beyond Modernism," 41.

4.2 Toyo Ito. Taichung Metropolitan Opera House in Taiwan (2005/2009–2016). Interior view of one of the two sets of spaces.

4.3 Toyo Ito. Taichung Metropolitan Opera House in Taiwan (2005/2009–2016). Interior view of the other set of spaces.

Not all sponge surfaces have the capacity to become architectural structures. Only those whose proportions and relational properties make them readily available to house a set of human activities (i.e., a program) can be translated realistically into full-fledged buildings.[4] That is, only a subset of these surfaces, otherwise originated within a purely geometric regime, features a specific physiognomy that *happens to intersect* the domain of architecture by virtue of being always already programmatic. Remarkably, Taichung is the first built instance of such an intersection.[5]

In evolving a building out of a perfectly regular geometric configuration, adjustments are necessary. In Taichung, such adjustments—especially those in plan—are taken right to the limit beyond which the original diagram would have been compromised. Given the drastic differences in scale of its programmatic components—notably between the small spaces required for offices, restaurant, and conference rooms, and the large spaces required for theaters and their equipment—an opera house does not lend itself very easily to being hosted within a periodic, cellular spatial arrangement whose legibility relies on self-similar repetition. Here, Ito's earlier Ghent program—featuring a narrower range of diverse scales for the activities occurring in the building—fitted more naturally into the articulation induced by the sponge surface. And yet, despite the significant deformations performed in Taichung, the original organizational model continues to exert itself, with its fundamental properties prevailing.

One of the indispensable modifications when turning a sponge surface into a building is to extend the horizontal tangent regions so as to obtain enough inhabitable floor area in between the vertical curved segments. This operation was rehearsed in Ghent and is enacted more decisively in Taichung, where the distances between the vertical segments that emerge from the floor and those

4. These relational properties concern the way in which the different spatial regions are connected to one another.

5. This building might be misread as evolving out of a so-called "minimal surface." A minimal surface is a special kind of sponge surface, with a homogeneous mean curvature equal to zero. Because of this singularity, load transmission across it runs through tensile and compressive membrane stresses alone. In other words, the surface's flexure is reduced to zero. Taichung was not conceived as a minimal surface.

that are sinking down are often so large that the perception of any tangency between them is lost. Using only this strategy, it was not possible to meet the required square footage, hence the additional insertion of planar floor slabs throughout. There are moments in which the slabs block some of the vertical cavities, and while they do not interfere with the systems of internal communication running through, at times they prevent such cavities from being used to introduce natural light. Still, the surface's porosity—an attribute that is central to the specific spatial relationships and phenomenology enabled by the sponge surface—remains very much present.

Programmatically, the geometric configuration from which Taichung stems can be understood on the basis of two types of spaces: *expansion areas* and *transition regions*. Expansion areas are sections—or rather, intersections—where the spatial continuum opens up both vertically and horizontally. The zones connecting two expansion areas constitute transition regions. Thus every expansion area is also the confluence of two or more transition regions. In the built structure, any of the programmatic spaces in between the vertical curved segments are transition regions, whereas those around the curved segments themselves are expansion areas. Where the transition regions are noticeably short—for instance, between a vertical cavity housing a staircase against the façade and the one on the closest corner of the big theater, readable on the second and third levels—their distinction from expansion areas becomes much less evident. It is in those moments that the spatial arrangement registers as a more compact articulation than the original kernel.

In the undistorted geometric model, vertical cavities are arranged along parallel and perpendicular axes. But in the distorted structure, most of them appear off-center, which occasionally hinders the reading of expansion areas and transition regions further. This is particularly apparent on the ground level. The original sponge surface was prone to being partitioned into functional volumes following the logic of cells or cell groups—that is, the kinds of self-similar areas that result from the regularly patterned placement of vertical units. The deformations in Taichung yield far more zoning possibilities, albeit at the expense of clearer readability. Yet to be seen is whether the former can be achieved without compromising the latter.

Taichung Opera House's least successful aspect may very well be its external appearance. Curtain walls, opaque enclosures varying in height and composition, circular openings, awkward corners, boxes popping up through the roof—it just seems as if there is too much going on, which alienates the simplicity of the initial idea: treating the outer planes as mere sections or cut lines, rather than faces or "façades." In this sense, the elevational clarity achieved in Ghent is missing in Taichung.

That said, *sponge buildings*—a term I use to generalize the typology inaugurated by Taichung—hold a compelling promise in terms of the relationship between outward manifestation and internal organization. Sponges in the natural world are singular formations, in that their ornamental pattern outside *is part of* their spatial arrangement inside. Analogously, the sponge building's identity lies between representational character and spatial disposition; between conditions of imageability and three-dimensional configuration.[6] These conditions do not "symbolize" or "express" anything happening on the inside. Rather, they *are* the inside. Distinguishing inside from outside in the sponge building is meaningless in an ontological sense as opposed to a rhetorical or purely perceptual one, which has been the case historically in architectural tropes such as "interior and exterior getting mixed up," "both domains flowing into each other," and so forth. The difference with the Venturian "duck" becomes obvious. The duck-envelope symbolizes the function of the building, but its defining qualities have nothing to do with the spatial arrangement of the interior.

In this regard, the sponge building cannot be reduced to the modern movement's outside-as-result-of-inside motto. Modern architects sought to achieve a particular kind of interior-exterior correspondence by treating an indepen-

6. The domain of "representation" in architecture operates primarily on two registers. The first alludes to a graphic or physical depiction (a floor plan, a model, etc.) that stands for an outside referent (a work of architecture) on which it is dependent and to which it is therefore subordinate. The second—the one I am invoking here—arises when a work of architecture, formerly a primary referent, becomes that which stands for another referent, whether internal or external to the work itself. In this case, the work *represents* values pertaining to a particular realm (e.g. political, social, vernacular, ethical, religious, etc.), and by embodying these values it acquires a certain *meaning*. As Sylvia Lavin noted, the phrase "representational character" may be made assimilable to Kevin Lynch's "imageability." See Sylvia Lavin, "Practice Makes Perfect," *Hunch* 11 (Winter 2006/7): 106.

dent plane—the façade—so that either program or interior volume (or both) might be legible from the outside. It was about *projecting* onto the outside wall in order to make it a display of the interior. In contrast, sponge buildings offer no independent enclosure in the first place; whatever is constitutive of the external condition of the building is equally constitutive of its three-dimensional articulation inside (fig. 4.4).

This essential dissimilarity between the two approaches can also be identified in the process of design thinking itself. In modern buildings, it is usually the interior that makes its way to the exterior. In sponge buildings, the whole structure is conceived as a three-dimensional arrangement with no predefined volumetric boundaries dissociating it *a priori* from an external field. The resulting outside condition is contingent upon the way that such an arrangement manifests itself relative to the specific volumetric envelope that is eventually given—as opposed to it being defined *independently*, or *sequentially afterward* so as to showcase the interior. If in modern architecture the plan was the generator, in sponge buildings it is rather a particular mode of subdividing space three-dimensionally that provides the originating situation.[7]

After the modern movement's advocacy of the façade as a display of the inside, and the Venturian duality of *building-as-spatial-organization* versus *building-as-representation* (faithfully endorsed by Koolhaas's "lobotomy" several years later), the sponge building suggests the beginning of a new paradigm: one that is certainly representational, but also spatial and programmatic.

7. The concept of *sponge* as suggested here stands in contradictory relationship to Sloterdijk's notion of *foam*. On the one hand, some examples of the former in building form might accommodate aspects of *co-isolation* that are essential to *foam*. *Sponge* and *foam* also share a pursuit of alternatives to both the Platonic solids, and ways of structuring space beyond columns and walls. On the other hand, however, pneumatic constructions and tensegrity systems—paradigmatic manifestations of foam for Sloterdijk—rarely, if ever, constitute sponge buildings. In addition, whereas emphasizing "the microcosmic intrinsic spatiality of each individual cell"—that is, privileging the individualism of the unit within a larger construct—is a fundamental foam premise, it is not a sponge one. See Peter Sloterdijk, *Sphären III. Schäume, Plurale Sphärologie* (Frankfurt: Suhrkamp Verlag, 2004), and Peter Sloterdijk, "Talking to Myself About the Poetics of Space," *Harvard Design Magazine* 30, no. 1 (Spring/Summer 2009), http://www.harvarddesign-magazine.org/issues/30/talking-to-myself-about-the-poetics-of-space. Accessed July 1, 2017.

Taken together, Taichung's various inconsistencies—involving deformations, additional slabs, spatial readability, and exterior appearance—are simply the result of a first stab at realizing such a paradigm. More important is the territory it delineates; a design territory that is, to date, largely uncharted.

4.4 Toyo Ito. Taichung Metropolitan Opera House in Taiwan (2005/2009–2016). Exterior view.

On Architecture's Metacriticality

The possibility of architecture being critical was severely attacked in the late 1990s and early 2000s.[1] Under the "post-critical" banner, the exhaustion of criticality was declared, its death proclaimed, and alternatives proposed.[2] This phenomenon cut across the humanities at large, and its echo is still very much felt today, when the related term "post-theory" is often heard in academia to describe the current state of affairs.[3] Around the mid-2000s,

1. Although this was by no means a new sentiment. Nearly a century ago Walter Benjamin claimed, "[f]ools lament the decay of criticism. For its day is long past. . . . It was at home in a world where perspectives and prospects counted and where it was still possible to adopt a standpoint. Now things press too urgently on human society." Walter Benjamin, "One-Way Street," in *Selected Writings, Volume 1: 1913–1926* (Cambridge, MA: Harvard University Press, 2004), 476.

2. Steven Maras provided a didactic insight into the relationship between the terms *critique*, *critical*, and *criticality* that is worth being quoted at the outset: "Criticality is that aspect of any approach or theory that imagines the work of critique, or sets out what it means to be critical in relation to an object, problem, or competing approach. Criticality has to do with imagining the limits of what is or is not critical. It relates to how critical approaches imagine acts of 'critical' reading and writing, and the way critical approaches take up politics in some ways and not others. Criticality is not so much the task of critiquing the critique, as teasing out the presuppositions of a critical/intellectual performance, and its identity conditions. So criticality has to do with the specific identity conditions of what a particular approach regards as critical, but also the broader way in which acts of criticism arrange discourse around them (set up opponents, imagine conflict or violence, think about the past or future, etc.)." In Steven Maras, "Communicating Criticality," *International Journal of Communication* 1 (2007): 167–86.

3. The assault on the critical has often gone hand in hand with an attack on theory, for reasons that well exceed the tradition of critical theory bringing the two realms together. It seems obvious, however, that their collapse does not apply *a priori*, although I shall not undertake to unpack this question in the context of this essay.

a counter-reaction arose within architectural discourse. Many raised their voices to argue for the necessity of recuperating the importance of critique: "the critical" in architecture needed to be resuscitated.

But perhaps critique never died—or even decayed, for that matter. Critical registers may have been in operation all through the so-called post-critical period. The critical landscape is vast enough; thus it seems hard to imagine that positions causing some kind of disciplinary impact—architectural or otherwise—were able to escape the wide diversity of forms that critical stances may take. Over the course of the twentieth century, critique was largely associated with critical theory and, more specifically, with Frankfurt School dialectics. Other discursive formations within which critical outlooks were effectively articulated include, as is well known, Marxist critique, New Criticism, the Chicago School, structuralism, queer theory, and several modes of deconstruction, to mention but a few. One might add those specific modes of critique that relied deliberately on immediate action and less so on exploiting intellectual content. The Dadaists' exacerbated mimicry, estrangement à la Brecht, and Guy Debord's *détournement* can be counted among those.[4]

A number of different situations, therefore, haunt post-critics. Inadvertently, they might have been enacting some former mode of critique. Or they might have engendered a few novel ones in their alleged getaway. Even more perversely, they might have unwittingly been re-enacting the very critical postures from which they were trying to move away, there potentially having been a dislodging of approach and target. To disentangle this discursive knot, and to see in what way critical regimes may have been at play within post-critical arguments, I shall discuss the lineage of criticality and post-criticality in architecture—with a focus on the American scene—within a wider theoretical context. For reasons yet to be explored, the question of the post-critical in architecture, as well as subsequent attacks on it, have commonly been shaped from within the discipline itself and in relation to architectural discourse alone.[5] It has not been the case in art history, for example, a field traditio-

4. Just a few years ago Hal Foster referred to some of these modes of critique. See Hal Foster, "Post-Critical," *October* 139 (January 2012): 3–8.

5. Of the authors writing from within the field of architecture, Reinhold Martin has perhaps been the only one who showed an interest in looking at the problem of critique outside the bound-

nally close to that of architecture. In art criticism, debates on the supposed exhaustion of the critical and ensuing arguments in favor of critique were raised around the same time as in the discipline of the built environment, yet with a marked tendency to stage the discussion within the broader domain of sociocultural theory.[6]

Critical, Post-Critical, Back to Critical

In his 1984 article "Critical Architecture: Between Culture and Form," K. Michael Hays posited critical architecture as one that operates dialectically between embodying a commentary on the pressing forces of culture and its formal autonomy. To make this argument, the American author staged an opposition between what he called "architecture as an instrument of culture" versus "architecture as autonomous form." In acknowledging culture as cause and content of built form, the former ended up being, for Hays, a sheer reification of sociocultural and sociopolitical values, an uncritical cultural manifestation. Conversely, the latter ignored culture altogether. The object's meaning was placed, instead, on the formal procedures originating the built form and its internal logic, and not on constituting a representation of the dominant culture. *Formalist* and *idealist* were qualifiers used by Hays to designate this position.[7]

Hays further postulated that the essence of the architectural work is saturated by both its condition as a historically contingent artifact and its "sensuous particularity"—that is to say, the specific aesthetic properties resulting from

aries of the field. However, he did so only to establish a general background of reference; he did not discuss the ontology of architectural critique in relation to contemporaneous critiques of sociocultural critique. See Reinhold Martin, "Critical of What? Toward a Utopian Realism," in *Constructing a New Agenda: Architectural Theory 1993-2009*, 1st ed. (New York, NY: Princeton Architectural Press, 2010), 346–62.

6. See, for instance, George Baker, Benjamin Buchloh, Hal Foster, Andrea Fraser, David Joselit, Rosalind Krauss, James Meyer, John Miller, Helen Molesworth, and Robert Storr, "Round Table: The Present Conditions of Art Criticism," *October* 100 (April 2002): 201–28.

7. "The temporal convention of interpretation here is that of an ideal moment in a purely conceptual space; architectural operations are imagined to be spontaneous, internalized—that is, outside circumstantial reality—and assimilable as pure idea." K. Michael Hays, "Critical Architecture: Between Culture and Form," *Perspecta* 21 (January 1984): 16.

its formal qualities. Consequently, for such an artifact to be critical, it ought to situate itself between resistance to culture as a body of self-reproducing and self-affirming principles, and to form as an internally generated system.[8] Hays finished his piece by commenting on the relationship between critical architecture (as a material reality) and architectural criticism (as discourse), another of critique's hobbyhorses. By occupying the liminal space between autonomous form and culture, critical architecture carries with it "ascertainable political and intellectual consequences," while criticism ought to asses cultural knowledge thus produced within a value system and determine the meaning of this system in accordance with the contingencies of a particular historical time.[9] Some commentators have coupled this responsibility with the necessity to identify, on the one hand, overarching shifts in direction on the part of practitioners, and on the other, aspects that have generally been neglected or overlooked in historical art practices.[10]

In addition to Hays, the figure of Peter Eisenman became paradigmatic in the American scene when the possibility of critical architecture was at stake.

8. It is worth noting the resonance of this formulation with more recent definitions of critical art, notably that of Jacques Rancière. Rancière added another layer to aesthetic form à la Hays, one regarding its relevance as a cultural decodifier capable of awakening audiences. He emphasized the capacity of critical form to build a certain awareness of the mechanisms of domination at play and, therefore, to turn otherwise passive spectators into active agents of transformation against those mechanisms. Such a contribution aside, Rancière's own description of the role of critical art did not fundamentally differ from Hays's predicate: "Critical art has to negotiate between the tension which pushes art towards 'life' as well as that which, conversely, sets aesthetics sensorarily apart from the other forms of sensory experiences." Jacques Racière, *Aesthetics and Its Discontents*, trans. Steven Corcoran (Cambridge: Polity Press, 2009), 46. By "life," Rancière refers to the sociopolitical sphere. I am granting the analogy between architecture and art on the basis of both realms sharing in the broader field of aesthetics within which Rancière is constructing his arguments.

9. Hays, "Critical Architecture," 27.

10. See Baker et al., "Round Table," 216, 219–20. On page 216, Krauss herself put it thus: "For me as a writer, criticism has always involved a more historical sense of shifts in direction of the large part of art practitioners. For example, the decision, at a certain point, on the part of a group of writers, that there was something called postmodernism to which one had to pay a great deal of attention, and postmodernism then took on a life of its own and rendered other forms of art making obsolete. So this sense of scanning the horizon for some new blip appearing on it, is part of what I've always assumed was the job of a critic." Rancière, for his part, would likely oppose this claim by arguing that there is no longer any solid background in relation to which such shifts can be counterposed. See Jacques Rancière, *The Emancipated Spectator*, trans. Gregory Elliott (London: Verso, 2010), 25.

Surprisingly, however, his discourse has commonly been conflated with that of Hays. Indeed, Eisenman committed himself to a life-long project of criticality, but one of a very different kind. Essentially, his undertaking consisted of recasting the understanding of architectural language as an autonomous system, one where meaning became restricted to the domain of syntactic relationships. In other words, he sought to remove all external meaning from the work of architecture to make its components refer only to themselves, thereby echoing early twentieth-century theories of non-objective art.[11] It is this kind of autonomy that he was specifically invested in. Therefore, Eisenman and Hays should not be lumped together. In fact, this seems obvious, since Eisenman argued for "architecture as autonomous form," which Hays rejected at the outset. If both authors advocated for "the critical," Eisenman limited himself to the aesthetic realm, while Hays weaved aesthetics and politics together.[12] Finally, Eisenman's theory was oppositional (subversive isolation by difference) and Hays operated through dialectical synthesis.[13]

"Post-critical" postures were then put together against a critical backdrop where Hays and Eisenman were the two salient figures. Some of those postures were associated with the resurgence of pragmatism around the turn of the century. For example, in his 1998 piece "A new Pragmatism," philosopher John Rajchman cast the power of the diagram as a way to interpret reality beyond the alleged negativity of critique. The use of the diagnostic (i.e., Foucauldian)/projective (i.e., Deleuzian) diagram would enable the creation of novel realms of possibility by linking the various realms driving contemporary life (e.g., networks, digital spaces, transnational flows), thus making

11. Wassily Kandinsky in particular comes to mind here. See Peter Eisenman, *Eisenman Inside Out: Selected Writings, 1963–1988* (New Haven, CN: Yale University Press, 2004).

12. Reinhold Martin arrived at a somewhat similar conclusion, although our formulations differ substantially. To his distinction within architecture between *political critique* (which he associates with authors like Manfredo Tafuri) and *aesthetic critique* (a phrase he attaches to Eisenman), I am nonetheless indebted. See Martin, "Critical of What? Toward a Utopian Realism," 350.

13. These terms have been confused all too often when mistakenly including Hays and Eisenman in the same critical category—for instance, in George Baird, "Criticality and Its Discontents," *Harvard Design Magazine* 21 (Fall/Winter 2004/2005): 16–17; and Robert Somol and Sarah Whiting, "Notes around the Doppler Effect and Other Moods of Modernism," in Krista Skyes (ed.), *Constructing a New Agenda: Architectural Theory 1993–2009*, 1st ed. (New York, NY: Princeton Architectural Press, 2010), 193.

way for an unprogrammable, unpredictable future. Rajchman did not seek to abandon criticality altogether, but rather to redefine it: "Perhaps in this way, the pragmatism of diagram and diagnosis might help transform the sense of what is critical in our thought and our work."[14] Other authors, such as Michael Speaks, had no trouble being overtly dismissive about criticality, and more generally about theory at large. Taking his cues from the integrated models of production behind business management systems, Speaks promoted what he termed "post-vanguard" professional practices defined by "design intelligence, and not by any formal, theoretical, or professional identity."[15]

Perhaps the post-critical position that gained most relevance was the one articulated by Robert Somol and Sarah Whiting in their 2002 piece titled "Notes Around the Doppler Effect and Other Moods of Modernism." Somol and Whiting asserted that, in recent decades, disciplinarity in Architecture, had been exhausted by the critical project, a discursive occurrence of which they were *critical*:

> For both [Eisenman and Hays], disciplinarity is presented as autonomy (enabling critique, representation, and signification), but not as instrumentality (projection, performativity, and pragmatics). One could say that their definition of disciplinarity is directed against reification, rather than towards the possibility of emergence.[16]

Somol and Whiting linked the critical project in architecture to a preoccupation to separate itself from the normative through the articulation of difference, as well as to indexicality,[17] opposition, "the belabored," and ultimately

14. John Rajchman, "A New Pragmatism?," in *Constructing a New Agenda*, 102.

15. Michael Speaks, "Design Intelligence Part 1: Introduction," *A+U Architecture and Urbanism* (2002): 10–18. Elsewhere he grounds his claim on the basis of the following alleged shifts: "If philosophy was the intellectual dominant of early twentieth century vanguards and theory the intellectual dominant of late twentieth century vanguards, then intelligence has become the intellectual dominant of twenty-first century post-vanguards. While vanguard practices are reliant on ideas, theories and concepts given in advance, post-vanguard practices are more entrepreneurial in seeking opportunities for innovation that cannot be predicted by any idea, theory or concept." Michael Speaks, "Design Intelligence Part 1: Introduction," in *Constructing a New Agenda*, 211.

16. Somol and Whiting, "Notes Around the Doppler Effect and Other Moods of Modernism," 193.

17. In their understanding, this term alludes to a ruse to combine materialism and significa-

"the difficult" and "the defined." Furthermore, they promoted an engagement with *the projective*, which referred to the pragmatism of instrumentalization, the embrace of multiplicity, "the performative," "the diagrammatic," "the atmospheric," and ultimately "the relaxed and easy."[18] Sylvia Lavin and Stan Allen joined the enterprise in rather similar terms. Claiming that architecture ceases to be "cool" when it clings to the critical tradition, Lavin suggested turning to "the ephemeral" and "the provisional"—as opposed to "the fixed" and "the durable" she associated with Modernism—for it could be a liberating and productive way to find new design possibilities.[19] Allen, for his part, advocated for "a form of practice committed to public legibility, to the active engagement of new technologies, and to creative means of implementation."[20]

Something worth noting begins to surface at this point. Post-critics repeatedly claimed to be opposing the criticality of both Hays's and Eisenman's projects. Nevertheless, post-critical positions wound up sounding all too close to one of the approaches Hays's "critical architecture" sought to overcome, namely that of "architecture as an instrument of culture." Therefore, were post-critics going unwittingly against themselves in confronting the very formulation of the critical into which their own was embedded? More ironically, did post-critical architecture exist before critical? Or, is it, rather, that the post-critical, despite appeals to "the projective," had something of a reactionary aspect to it in that it named an approach that had first been identified and then challenged around eighteen years earlier?:

> The first position [architecture as an instrument of culture] emphasizes culture as the cause and content of built form; the task of the interpreter, then, becomes the study of objects and environments as signs, symptoms, and instruments of cultural values. On this view architecture is essentially an epiphenomenon, dependent on socioe-

tion, namely, to render architecture, through built form, a hypostatization of its own process of becoming.

18. Somol and Whiting, "Notes Around the Doppler Effect and Other Moods of Modernism," 193.

19. Lavin in lectures delivered during the spring semester of 2004 at Harvard, Princeton, and the University of Toronto. I borrowed the reference from Baird, "Criticality and Its Discontents," 19.

20. Stan Allen, "Stocktaking 2004: Nine Questions About the Present and Future of Design," *Harvard Design Magazine* 20 (Spring/Summer 2004): 16.

conomic, political, and technological processes for its various states and transformations.[21]

A number of critics reacted promptly after the post-critical wave. George Baird could not make sense of the fact that the "relaxed" and "easy," while clearly at odds with the "difficult," supposedly cannot be reconciled with "resistance." In addition, he warned that, without a body of "projective theory" with which to measure the capacity for social transformation of putatively post-critical forms of practice, architecture could "easily again find itself conceptually and ethically adrift" and at risk of falling into past formats of the "merely" pragmatic and the "merely" decorative.[22] Reinhold Martin feared quite plainly that in the name of the post-critical all forms of critique might be evacuated from the domain of architecture.[23]

After this brief account of the problem of the critical in recent American discourse, and before moving on to discussing the issue within a larger theoretical framework, a few more questions arise that should be noted. The voices reclaiming a space for critique after post-critical debates assumed the demise of what they were trying to recuperate, since otherwise there would be nothing to recuperate in the first place. Yet this alleged "death" is fictitious on account of the following two points. For one thing, it would appear easy to prove that, given the marked theoretical undercurrent of some of the post-critical arguments—especially that of Somol and Whiting—criticality as such, which they were challenging, was indissolubly built into the very craft of their own theoretical armature.[24] Second, architectural design kept operating cri-

21. Hays, "Critical Architecture," 16.

22. Baird, "Criticality and Its Discontents," 21.

23. "[B]y what criteria is the 'post-critical' asking to be judged, beyond mere acceptance an accommodation of existing societal, economic, or cultural norms? . . . [J]ust what sort of world they [projective practitioners of the post-critical] are projecting and affirming in their architecture and in their discourse?" Martin, "Critical of What? Toward a Utopian Realism," 349, 359. Martin attempted to provide an answer to his own question by championing a revised version of criticality—one based on the notion of "utopian realism."

24. I shall not elaborate this argument further, as my doing so would exceed the scope of this essay. A discussion of the relationship between theory and the possibility of its being critical would, once again, be required here. For a brilliant elucidation of this and related matters, see Louis Althusser, *Philosophy and the Spontaneous Philosophy of the Scientists & Other Essays* (London: Verso, 1990).

tically regardless of any theoretical articulations, an occurrence not hard to discern through Hays's formulation. He chose Mies Van Der Rohe's buildings to illustrate his claim that architecture may be considered critical when its *raison d'être* is to be found at the intersection "between culture as a massive body of self-perpetuating ideas and form supposedly free of circumstance."[25] One of the most successful ways in which this strategic placement can be achieved, Hays added, was through repetition. As apparent in Mies's *oeuvre*, his architectural propositions would not fundamentally change from project to project—they were merely rearticulated based on built-up experience and changing circumstances. "Repetition thus demonstrates how architecture can resist, rather than reflect, an external cultural reality," Hays wrote.[26] It is in this particular sense that Hays and Eisenman can be discussed together, for the former would likely agree that the latter's work can be described as "resistant by repetition."

Did the sort of architecture Hays talked about cease to exist altogether with the advent of the post-critical? What happened to architectural production vis-à-vis its potential critical power over the past twenty years? To what extent are all those architects whose work is harshly criticized because of their tendency to "repeat themselves" actually being genuinely critical—even if implicitly? Might Zaha Hadid Architects—one of the current stereotypes of an uncritical office—turn out to be, in some sense, a model for a critical designer?

The central problem, however, remains to determine what has fundamentally shifted throughout this alternating discursive battle—if anything at all. I shall hold off on possible answers to this and the related questions I posed earlier, as I do not wish to rush to conclusions while within disciplinary boundaries. Let us first scan one of the fields in which the possibility of critique in a wider sense has been most consistently explored: that of sociocultural theory.

25. Hays, "Critical Architecture," 22.

26. Ibid., 27. Here we would find Rancière on the same page—it is the *strangeness* built into forms that follow to a large degree their own logic (i.e., Mies's architectural schemes being re-enacted in diverse situations), rather than "dissolving appearances" by reifying exiting cultural conditions, which enables such forms to *resist*. See Rancière, *Aesthetics and Its Discontents*, 45.

Displacing Ideology Critique

Among writings in western humanities and social sciences that have been rethinking the nature of ideology critique in recent times, the works of Jacques Rancière, Peter Sloterdijk, Slavoj Žižek, and Bruno Latour are especially pertinent for the purposes of this essay. For one thing, the schemes put forward by these authors relative to the articulation of criticality, as I interpret them, feature a number of common traces that make them particularly prone to being read together, thereby pointing to a shift that exceeds the relevance of individual positions. Second, as I shall show, those common traces resonate in distinctively productive ways with the core aspects of architectural criticality discussed above.

In his *Critique of Cynical Reason* (1983), Sloterdijk saw "cynicism," both on the personal and the institutional levels, as the dominant paradigm in the operating cultural modalities of contemporary times. As an effective counterattack strategy, he suggested recuperating the tradition of "kynicism." Traditionally, ideology critique sought to identify—and ultimately collapse—the distance between so-called "social reality" and our representation of it. In other words, the goal of a critique was to render legible our alleged false consciousness of reality. In the more sophisticated version of the Frankfurt School, ideology critique not only attempted to show "the way things really are," but to prove that social reality cannot reproduce itself without so-called "ideological mystification"—i.e., ideological distortion is written into the very ontology of reality's self-reproduction. Thus, by claiming that today ideology's dominant mode of functioning is cynical, Sloterdijk posed the subject inducing ideological control as one that, while aware of the distance between fake appearance and reality, still insists on feeding appearances. To put it differently: through cynical reason—responsible for yielding an "enlightened false consciousness," in Sloterdijk's terminology—the subjects acts in such a way that they are perfectly conscious of the falsehood at play, and yet do not renounce the interest hidden behind a specific ideological imperative. Faced with this shift, Sloterdijk expressed his doubts as to the dismantling power of ideology critique:

> Cynicism is *enlightened false consciousness*. It is that modernized, unhappy consciousness, on which enlightenment has labored

> both successfully and in vain. It has learned its lessons in enlightenment, but it has not, and probably was not able to, put them into practice. Well-off and miserable at the same time, this consciousness no longer feels affected by any critique of ideology; its falseness is already reflexively buffered.[27]

Žižek, on the other hand, was not so pessimistic upon confronting Sloterdijk's thesis. Ideology critique cannot cease to be operational, since, whether traditional or now driven by cynical reason, ideology still structures society itself. For Žižek, it is a matter of changing the defining traits of ideology critique based on the fact that "symptomatic reading"—i.e., confronting an ideological text or a situation with "its blank spots, with what it must repress to organize itself, to preserve its consistency"—is no longer effective against a "cynical reason [that] takes this distance into account in advance."[28] Lies ought not to be challenged simply as such, but as lies that claim natural truth, as lies assuming their being taken seriously in the first place.

Alternatively, Sloterdijk's antidote against his diagnosis was to go back to what he called "kynicism." The typical kynical sentiment involves the popular—if not "plebeian"—rejection of the official ruling ideology by means of everyday sarcasm and irony. Kynical reason attempts to expose what lies behind the apparently noble, solemn tone of ideological phrases—such as will to power and personal interests—by way of mocking and ridiculing them. It thereby targets the discourse and speech of specific people, such as those of especially contested politicians. Žižek's reservations about this kind of reaction were grounded in it being "more pragmatic than argumentative," for it "subverts the official proposition by confronting it with the situation of its enunciation."[29] The *a priori* helplessness of kynicism, for Žižek, stems from the fact that the way in which kynical subversion seeks to reduce ideological distance is already taken into account by the cynical reason enacting ideology.

27. Peter Sloterdijk, *Critique of Cynical Reason*, trans. Michael Eldred (Minneapolis: University of Minnesota Press, 1987), 5.

28. Slavoj Žižek, *The Sublime Object of Ideology* (London/New York: Verso, 1989), 30.

29. Ibid., 29.

In my view, kynical procedures may also be seen in the light of a broader Sloterdijkian prospect, namely, his advocacy of proximity, his urge to "get to the facts" when it comes to establishing the possibility of critique. Echoing Benjamin's dictum that "grand views" of the whole are no longer possible in a world where multiple perspectives apply, Sloterdijk called for "a stance of extreme closeness" and "proper proximity," instead of "proper distance" and elevated critiques aiming for overviews. The German philosopher associated these precepts with the term *concernedness* (*Betroffenheit*), as the quality of "being concerned" that gives rise to a particular kind of critique when things have gotten too close for comfort for us.[30]

More recently, Bruno Latour arrived at a somewhat similar bottom line by following a different argumentative path, probably under Sloterdijk's influence. In his 2004 essay "Why Has Critique Run Out of Steam? From Matters of Fact to Matters of Concern," Latour built a critique of critique centered upon the premise that discursive critique has by and large operated on two different levels. On the one hand, it sought to show that "things" to which people feel attached (in a Latourian sense, anything from poetry, to Gods, religion, or proteins) do nothing "by themselves," and therefore all those attachments are only fetishes, which is to say, projections of the subject's desires onto the object. Criticism here is therefore equated with anti-fetishism. On the other hand, the critic has habitually sought to illustrate that what people "think" and "do" is in fact entirely determined by the action of causalities which, intrinsic to social reality, appear concealed to the "naïve believer"—this simply being Latour's version of traditional ideology critique. In this second scenario, the loser is the subject. Naïve believers are haunted by the "critical barbarian" who is obsessed with making them see all those meta-relationships of which they are unaware, while the object itself receives little to no attention. For this reason, it is no wonder that eventually critique "ran out of steam":

> Is it so surprising, after all, that with such positions given to the object, the humanities have lost the hearts of their fellow citizens, that they had to retreat year after year, entrenching themselves always further in the narrow barracks left to them by more and more

30. See Sloterdijk, *Critique of Cynical Reason*, xxxiii.

> stingy deans? The Zeus of Critique rules absolutely, to be sure, but over a desert.[31]

What made Latour uncomfortable in this situation was the fact that the same suspicious attitude, the same urge to question and criticize, the same anti-fetishistic impulse was not applied either to the discursive structures wherein hidden causalities determining human demeanors were commonly framed (sociology, economics, semiotics, conspiracy theory, or whatever the specific field of study happens to be), or to the things that critics themselves cherished the most, the things that were closest to them, the things they really considered worthwhile "matters of concern" (most notably criticism itself, but also their own objects of desire and, I would add, they themselves as critics). In the former case critics fell into sheer positivism, whereas in the latter they exhibited a kind of "sturdy realism." Latour, then, did not propose to derive the "new critical tools" he wished to put forward by becoming "anti-fetishistic" about everything critics had commonly not targeted critically, or by dismantling "critical weapons so uncritically built up by our predecessors."[32] Instead, he suggested a shift in direction altogether. Rather than constructing critiques of "matters of fact" (what is generally taken for granted, what appears "given") by moving away from them so as to pin down the conditions that make them possible (i.e., ideologies), Latour advocated for questioning the "matters of fact" themselves in the first place by getting closer to them. In his own terminology, this reversal of an outward movement into an inward one changes the status of "matters of fact," now regarded as "matters of concern." The parallel with Sloterdijk is already evident enough: let us recall here his invocation of "extreme closeness" through "concernedness."

Latour went on to propose a specific way to enact this proximity, one that revealed his constructionist inclinations. Waving the flag of empiricism and realism, he promoted a critical attitude, not aimed at dismantling things, but at adding reality to them—which is to say, at assembling (initially) matters of fact into the constellations of other "things" (their "aura," their web of associations with other structures such as discourses, disciplines, peoples,

31. Bruno Latour, "Why Has Critique Run Out of Steam? From Matters of Fact to Matters of Concern," *Critical Inquiry* 30 (Winter 2004): 239.

32. Ibid., 243.

etc.) that they mobilize, if not necessitate, by virtue of their very existence. In other words, new modes of critique, for Latour, ought to focus not on a withdrawal that hypothetically leads to a vantage point, but on constructing the cosmology of discursive objects that are relevant to things by means of addressing the things themselves—now rendered highly complex, historically situated matters of concern. Critique would then be about more, not about less; about association and multiplication, as opposed to subtraction. It is the critic's responsibility to perform the activity of "gathering" objects through objects; he is "not the one who debunks, but the one who assembles."[33]

Strongly resonating with some of the principles advanced by Sloterdijk and Latour, Rancière's critique of critique emerges in his *The Emancipated Spectator* of 2009. Rancière submitted that the concepts and frameworks of traditional critical thinking still exist, yet their current usage exposes a complete inversion of their original orientation and ends. To illustrate this claim, he performed a detailed reading of a number of images that, conceived within the domains of art and photography, were meant to activate an otherwise critically passive spectator. According to Rancière, those kinds of images were supposed to produce a twofold effect. On the one hand, they were to raise an awareness about systems of domination behind the appearance of everyday objects. On the other hand, they were to create a feeling of complicit guilt in the spectator, of the kind "here is the obvious reality you do not want to see, because you know you are responsible for it"[34]—a cynical reason à la Sloterdijk, but now folded back upon the avowedly dominated. What Rancière primarily wanted to show was that the distance between appearance and reality necessary for critique to be effective is no longer in place, since what we understand as reality has also become a spectacle of itself. Demonstrators, who are out on the streets because they consumed certain kinds of imagery—for example, the destruction of the Twin Towers staged as the collapse of the spectacle and the commodity law—offer us yet another consumable spectacle in their very process of urban self-deployment. Resistance is turned into sign, thus entering the dynamics of commodity exhibition it was meant to denounce.

33. Ibid., 246.

34. Rancière, *The Emancipated Spectator*, 27.

Based on political leaning, Rancière then interpreted the impotence of criticism when confronting that vicious circle in a different way. The Left adopts a melancholy attitude—if not plain cynicism, yet again—by claiming that, not only are there no alternatives to the dominance of "the beast," but in fact we are satisfied with this being the case. On the other hand, the Right warns us that the more we attempt to combat "the beast," the more we are feeding its triumph over us. The reversal, therefore, lies in the fact that, where formerly critical mechanisms sought to reveal the commodity law behind appearances in order to "arm combatants in the social struggle," now they do the exact opposite; for example, they feed the very ideology they were intended to dismantle. Not only does information not trigger activation in principle; not only is exposure to "truths," Rancière sought to prove, not enough to incite reaction. Rather, today it is quite the contrary, for the mere existence of these images is not revolutionary but simply evidence of our own self-awareness.

Thus, a fundamental disconnection has established itself between critical procedures and their original purpose, one that precipitates in a twofold manner. For one thing, it renders traditional critical frameworks completely ineffective in the face of current global capitalism; and, second, it annihilates the possibility of any critique of critique that envisions to further invert the logic of "appearance versus reality" by taking the form of re-examining either its genealogy, concepts, and procedures in themselves, or the way in which these became intertwined with social constructions. Latour already pointed out that, while critics have spent years trying to disclose the prejudices behind apparently objective claims, "we now have to reveal the real objective and incontrovertible facts behind the *illusion* of prejudices."[35] Rancière's description of the problem of critique's critique very much recalls the formulation of his compatriot:

> There is thus clearly a dialectic inherent in the denunciation of the critical paradigm: it proclaims the obsolescence of the latter only to reproduce its mechanism; to transform the ignorance of reality or the denial of misery into ignorance of the fact that reality and misery have disappeared; to transform the desire to ignore what makes us

35. Latour, "Why Has Critique Run Out of Steam? From Matters of Fact to Matters of Concern," 227.

guilty into the desire to ignore the fact that there is nothing we need feel guilty about.[36]

Similar to Latour, Rancière sought a way out by means of sidestepping the conundrum, rather than by tackling it and recomposing it. He suggested destabilizing the foundation of the traditional critical logic by considering a number of subversive aspects: namely, that those who do not seem capable (the putatively "dominated") might actually be so; that a somehow hidden social apparatus, which presumably has them trapped in their condition and keeps transforming reality into image, ought not be taken for granted; and that an alleged "beast" absorbing all desires and energies into its unfathomable workings should not be presupposed. Rancière posited the resultant space as one of "dissensus." Here, a single, homogeneous mode of representation and interpretation, rooted in the assumption of a reality concealed behind appearances, is no longer in place. Instead, situations are construed as emerging differently in different times and places.

If Latour held a constructionist view of the critic whereby he would approach "the thing itself" and, through it, he would assemble constellations of other "things," Rancière encouraged us to see that "every situation can be cracked open from the inside, reconfigured in a different regime of perception and signification."[37] Altering what can be seen and thought (his well-known notion of the "distribution of the sensible") might result in a rearticulation of the disposition of capacities and the field of the possible—a power Rancière fostered over the hopeless search for unmasking fetishes and the unconscious validations of the haunting presence of "the other."

Toward a Critical Constructionism in Architecture

How can one profitably read this shift within the field of sociocultural theory regarding the problem of critique in relation to the alternations in architectural debates on criticality I presented above? My contention is that, in some of

36. Rancière, *The Emancipated Spectator*, 30.

37. Ibid., 49.

their central aspects, the post-critical discourses in architecture engendered around the turn of the century were rather close to the new critical tenets espoused by the authors I just discussed. This being the case, it would follow that architectural post-critical formulations were in some sense "critical,"[38] although with a few reservations. Let us unfold this argument.

For one thing, being critical by resistance, akin to Hays, might indeed be considered obsolete. Sloterdijk would object that such a plain resisting attitude is blind to the cynicism at play; Latour would problematize architecture being critical about something else yet not about itself *qua* discursive structure; and Rancière would hold that, in resisting culture, architecture is turning itself into the very spectacle it tries to denounce. In other words, the fact that the end originally targeted operates according to different dynamics at present would render Hays's version of critical architecture simply ineffective. Second, it now appears evident that the post-critical turn had a marked constructionist element linking it to the direction in which the critiques of sociocultural critique I have examined were pointing. In post-critical terms, form was not construed in its capacity to "resist" but in its potential to "construct," in the sense of "enabling emergence" by "embracing" and "projecting." These prospects no doubt resonate with the ideas of "assembling" in Latour and "reconfiguring" in Rancière. Even the call for "proximity," for "getting to the facts" that was shared by all three thinkers, seemed to be echoed in the promotion of "pragmatism"—and, on some level, of "instrumentalization" as well—that was characteristic of post-critical agendas. In this sense, one

38. In fact, post-critical frameworks, understood as knowledge structures, are *always already* critical. Equating post-critical with non-critical—as has often been the case—is deceptive, despite apparent hints in that direction on the part of post-critics themselves. If criticality is understood as the realm of possibility within which a critical or intellectual performance and its identity conditions may play out, then there is no reason why the post-critical cannot be construed as a mode of criticality in and of itself. It could be objected that the post-critical relates to the intellectual but not the critical, this being the whole problematic around it. However, that is not the case, for post-critical postures are relational *in principle*, which means they cannot be articulated unless in relation to the critical, on which they comment and, in fact, *critique*. Therefore, any discursive position articulated against the critical inevitably falls back into the critical realm. Within this general principle, what follows is a discussion of the specific case of post-critical formulations in contemporary architectural discourse, namely, of the particularities of their critical thrust as revealed by comparison to shifts in contemporary modes of critique within the field of sociocultural theory.

could speak of a certain post-critical realism that bore the traces of the one championed particularly by Latour.

Admittedly, this line of reasoning seems to be at odds with the claim I made earlier that post-critical discourses ended up on the verge of turning architecture into a sheer instrument of culture, and in fact here is where a warning must be given. "Post-critical gathering" was promoted along the lines of accommodating cultural, social, and economic norms by means of adjusting. That is to say, the object (in this case, architecture) would assemble by taking in other objects to which it would have no trouble adapting: "as a means of defining architecture's field or discipline, a Doppler architecture acknowledges the adaptive synthesis of architecture's many contingencies."[39] Such an inward dynamic, where the object is a mere recipient, stands in contrast to the outward movement that was to be triggered, rather, through the object and towards rearticulating that which is being "embraced." In other words, for a constructionist approach to be critical there ought to be a restructuration of the outside in operation. For Latour, a consideration of architecture as a matter of concern—i.e., as a contested, questioned reality—may only occur by way of creating a cluster of external associations inextricably connected to the fact that it is architecture, as opposed to anything else; the object serving as a catalyst in the first place. For Rancière, constructing a space of "architectural dissensus" would entail a destabilization, the eventual redistribution of the sensible, the alteration of what is possible in external regimes of perception and signification (what can be felt and thought) as a resulting effect from cracking architecture open from the inside. In general, it is not clear to me that this subversive will to affect other domains was present in the way post-critical frameworks were formulated. Perhaps only Rajchman's view, in his positing the diagram as a tool for engendering novel realms of possibility by means of reinterpreting architectural realities, came close to reproducing—or, in fact, anticipating, given the applicable chronology—both Latour's and Rancière's prospects somewhat faithfully.

A kind of *zeitgesty* sensibility hovers above post-critical discourses in architecture when read against a significant set of theories of critique put forward in the humanities and the social sciences. As I have shown, some of the

39. Somol and Whiting, "Notes Around the Doppler Effect and Other Moods of Modernism," 196.

core aspects structuring the post-critics' agendas reverberate quite clearly with those of new critical frameworks being fostered in those fields, even if post-critics themselves made no noteworthy metadiscursive references. Consequently, the hypothesis advanced at the outset holds; namely, that cases being made for recuperating critique after the advent of post-critical arguments were based on a fallacious premise, for those proved to possess—albeit inadvertently—a rather promising critical drive. Differently put: there was nothing to reclaim. The post-critical was but an unconscious tag for another mode of criticality, even if the job was only half-done.

The more suspicious version of this diagnosis would have it that, in fact, there was nothing unconscious about it, for, in good cynical fashion, the post-critical was merely a false flag to cover up the true critical operation at play. Following this argument, post-critics would have been knowingly putting an ideology to work with a view to obscuring the very nature of their project. Be that as it may, what seems more relevant here is to highlight the hopeful seed underwriting post-critical ventures, since it might be turned into an effective critical paradigm. To do so, rather than mourning the alleged "loss of the critical," efforts ought to point in the direction of theorizing the possibility of a critical constructionism in architecture—that is, beyond the merely "projective." At the level of discourse, such a project would entail accounting for architecture's destabilizing capacities, namely, the ways in which architecture as a discursive structure might induce knowledge of external sociocultural dynamics, rather than merely translating them into its code. At the level of design, the same enterprise would make it necessary to specifically determine how the rearticulation of external domains is possible through the "gathering power" of the particularities of architectural practice.

Critical Imageability

Charles Jencks was right when he predicted that "the iconic building is here to stay."[1] Its generalization and expansion in the form of so-called "image architecture" has become central to the way cities are being shaped across the world. Since the early 2010s, the phenomenon of image architecture has been joined by another essentially based around similar tenets, if often adjusted to a rhetoric of economic modesty and smaller scales: the versions of postmodernism currently present in biennales, architecture schools, and practice, in Europe and the US alike.[2] Emphasizing graphics, style recycling, and questions of *shape*—whilst mostly void of the deeper social and cultural agenda underpinning the original postmodernism—these twenty-first century instantiations reinforce what we can understand as a representational break grounded in a duality between *building-as-representation* and *building-as-spatial-organization*, where the domains delineated by each term are *a priori* independent. This divide also lies at the core of image architecture, which for this reason alone can be regarded as a fundamentally postmodernist trend. Indeed, it is no coincidence that Jencks, the champion of postmodernism *par excellence*, addressed image architecture with such interest around the mid-2000s.[3]

1. In a debate held at Columbia University on October 26, 2005.

2. The first two Chicago Biennials, UCLA, and discourses around practices in the Belgian and Italian scenes can be cited here as representative examples.

3. See Charles Jencks, *The Iconic Building* (New York, NY: Rizzoli, 2005).

Despite its widespread use in architectural discourse, the term "representation" is not often sufficiently understood to operate simultaneously on two different semantic register. The first alludes to a graphic or physical depiction (a floor plan, a model, etc.) that stands for an outside referent (a work of architecture) on which it is dependent, and to which it is therefore subordinate. The second arises when a work of architecture, formerly a primary referent, becomes that which stands for another, whether internal or external to the work itself. In this case, the work *represents* values pertaining to a particular realm (e.g. political, social, vernacular, ethical, or religious), and by embodying any number of these values it acquires a certain meaning. Symbolism, ornament, adornment, and related notions around the question of signification typically fall into this register, which shall be the object of discussion here.

Though rather old in its embodiment in built form, the duality of building-as-representation and building-as-spatial-organization had a defining moment in *Learning from Las Vegas*. In the introductory paragraphs of "Ugly and Ordinary Architecture, or the Decorated Shed," Robert Venturi, Denise Scott Brown, and Steven Izenour (VSBI) refer to the "duck" and the "decorated shed" as "manifestations" of the same attribute, namely the lack of consistency, the "contradictions" that may be exploited between, on the one hand, "form, structure and program," and on the other, "symbolic and representational elements."[4] While typically construed as different, this suggests that the notions of the duck and the decorated shed in fact share the same ethos.

For this realization to be productive, such an ethos ought to be explored by analyzing the relations between those sets of aspects whose contradictions VSBI wish to exploit. When constructing the definition of duck and decorated shed, they added 3) "shape" or "overall symbolic form"—more recently captured by the term "envelope"—to 1) "system of space, structure, and program" and 2) "representational elements." In the decorated shed, the representational elements are applied independently of the other two; signs are deployed on a plane that is either physically or compositionally detached from a generic, representationally mute shape. The duck, conversely, features an enve-

4. Robert Venturi, Denise Scott Brown, and Steven Izenour, *Learning from Las Vegas: The Forgotten Symbolism of Architectural Form* (Cambridge, MA: MIT Press, 1977), 87.

lope whose very three-dimensional profile constitutes the representational element itself, resulting in what the authors called "building-becoming-sculpture." In the decorated shed, a rapport between the nature of the "system of space, structure, and program" and the representational character of the building is inexistent.[5] Yet, similarly, the definition of the system in the duck remains basically unaffected by the nature of the representational element: it merely becomes "distorted."[6]

Implications follow on two levels. Firstly, a description of the internal spatial arrangement that might be made to correspond to the model of either the duck or the decorated shed is never provided. What would a section or an axonometric drawing of the inside of the duck look like? One is left to believe that this matter is irrelevant to the authors. Instead, their theory emphasizes image, and therefore the conditions of interiority could be of any kind.[7] Secondly, a careful study of the array of instances given in *Learning from Las Vegas* reveals that such a distortion of the system of space alludes, in fact, solely to the exterior, which is to say, to the effect of a duck-like profile (as opposed to a box-like one) on the three-dimensional contour area of the building, whether the profile be exemplified by that of a cross-shaped Gothic cathedral or a hamburger stand in Dallas.[8] In other words, the internal spatial arrangement of a duck and a decorated shed may very well be identical; for example, one based on a floor-upon-floor sequence or a single empty space. In other words, the duck is fundamentally a shed in the overall shape (i.e., volumetric outline) of a particular animal species.

Epistemologically, what this analysis shows is that both the concept of the duck and that of the decorated shed rest on the basis of the representational break. Accordingly, whether a building is characterized as a duck or a shed, it will embody the duality of building-as-representation versus building-as-spatial-organization and will therefore revert back to the same old tradition.

5. The phrase "representational character," as Sylvia Lavin pointed out, can be assimilated with Kevin Lynch's "imageability" and Charles Jencks's "iconicity." See Sylvia Lavin, "Practice Makes Perfect," *Hunch, the Berlage Institute Report* no. 11 (2007): 106.

6. Venturi, Scott Brown, and Izenour, *Learning from Las Vegas*, 87.

7. Ibid.

8. Ibid., 105, 113.

That said, while essentially keeping with this tradition, *Learning from Las Vegas* prompted an exploitation of the duality to such new levels of intensity and variety that it originated a shift of exceptional proportions. As opposed to any number of historical cases—such as, say, neoclassical architecture—where the representational dimension of a building specifically referenced a codified stylistic format (the conventions of classical language)—VSBI extended the representational content to virtually any imageable vocabulary: that of a Renaissance temple, the profile of a sausage, commercial signage, etc. In so doing, they extended the range of the first term of the duality, building-as-representation. At the same time, in proposing a deliberate manipulation of the disagreements between the two terms, they further fueled the schism between them. As a result, the representational possibilities enabled by VSBI's extreme exploitation of the duality are indeed exponentially greater, but so is the gap with respect to spatial organization.

Consequences of the "Bilbao Effect"

In the years following *Learning from Las Vegas*, the original postmodernism—in the representational sense relevant here—moved by and large away from its initial purpose, thereby anticipating in some respects the re-enactments presently being witnessed. Its initial commitment to the integration of buildings into the urban realm by way of engaging a wider public (in contrast to distant, self-alienating modern language) ended up evolving into largely insubstantial, glib decoration. A considerable part of the production of the 1970s and early 1980s found itself trapped in what was labeled as Historicist Postmodernism, a stylistic fad that embraced the use of conventions pertaining to earlier time periods. Triggered by the Guggenheim Museum in Bilbao, Spain, it was only a quarter of a century after VSBI laid the discursive foundations for a particularly acute exploitation of the representational break that it started to be fully implemented. With the completion of Gehry's building, the question of *imageability* (understood here as the region of possibility within which a work of architecture may powerfully resonate with the subject's faculty to form and interpret mental images), as well as related issues of meaning, acquired renewed weight—the effects of which are still being experienced in their entirety today.[9]

The importance of what Gehry's building brought about for the city of Bilbao is well known.[10] To be sure, Jørn Utzon's Opera House had similarly put Sydney on the map twenty-five years earlier, while Philip Johnson and John Burgee's AT&T building in New York may have received comparable attention in the press. Yet it was Gehry's titanium construction that brought on an explosion of image architecture. In the context of globalization's tendency for borderlessness, the fixity of codified architectural styles has been replaced by code-free icons, capable of being at once representationally potent while flexible enough to host a diverse array of semantic associations. The main purpose of the most ambitious examples of image architecture is defined by a strong demand for instant fame and economic prosperity, which are entrusted to the attention-grabbing qualities of imageability. Two examples that followed on from the success of Gehry's Guggenheim, both completed in 2003, can be cited as cases in point: the Kunsthaus in Graz by Peter Cook and Colin Fournier, and the Selfridges Department Store by Future Systems (fig. 6.1).

The Return of Debates on Representation in the Twenty-First Century

Following the Bilbao Effect, a diversification of architectural strategies resonating at the level of imageability occurred that expanded to a broader range of scales and programs than that of Gehry's building, reaching an unprecedented peak during the first decade of the twenty-first century. Given this outburst, a significant section of international architectural discourse was shaped accordingly, culminating around the mid-2000s with a number of

9. I am adjusting the definition of the term "imageability" to the case of architecture. The original definition alluded to "any physical object," although it was intended specifically for the city. See Kevin Lynch, *The Image of the City* (Cambridge, MA: M.I.T. Press, 1960), 9. It is also worth comparing my redefinition to Anthony Vidler's use of the term when alluding to Reyner Banham's discussion of the concept of image in his *The New Brutalism* piece. See Anthony Vidler, "Toward a Theory of the Architecture Program," *October* 106 (Fall 2003): 70.

10. Due to the significant volume of visitors attracted from outside the Basque region, the museum generated, in as little as two years, enough money to finance another four Guggenheims. This economic dynamic seduced an overwhelming number of foreign entrepreneurs who went to the northern Spanish city to invest, greatly boosting the region's fortune. The extensive media coverage, however, turned Bilbao's Guggenheim into something more than just a local success. For a more elaborate discussion regarding this building's impact on the city of Bilbao, see Jencks, *The Iconic Building*.

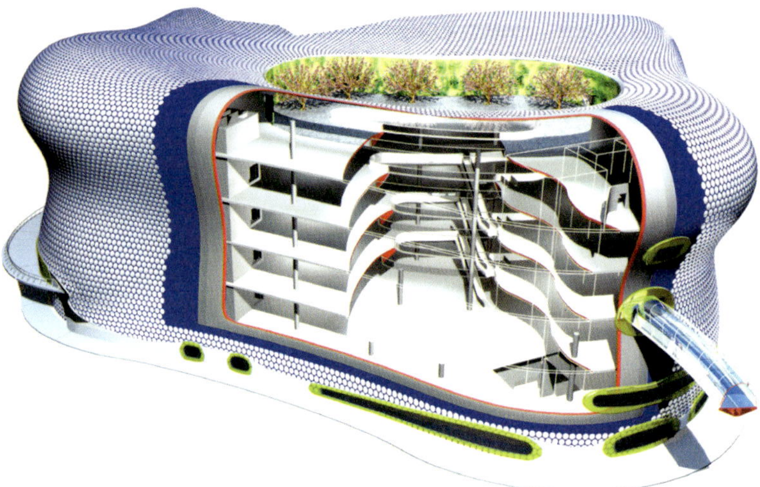

6.1 Future Systems. Selfridges Department Store in Birmingham, UK (1999–2003). Normative spatial organization as infill for singular envelope.

writings by Jencks and Alejandro Zaera-Polo, as well as the eleventh issue of *Hunch*, titled "Rethinking Representation."

A close reading of this 2007 issue of *Hunch* reveals the same dynamic playing out everywhere today: namely, that despite their growing elaborateness, the representational concept-operations driving image architecture tend to target issues of envelope, surface, outline, and graphics, while leaving spatial organizations fundamentally unquestioned. Editor Penelope Dean structured the issue around ten terms that she called "representational labels," each distilled from a piece by a different contributor.[11] For example, under the "Apply" label, John McMorrough wrote about how the application of two-dimensional painting can be utilized as a means to alter the perception of three-dimensional space. To illustrate this, McMorrough resorted to the phenomenon of Supergraphics that developed during the late 1960s and early 1970s, as well as some of the works by Venturi and Scott Brown, such as their 1962 Grands Restaurant in Philadelphia.[12] Under "Enlarge," Dean herself addressed the ways in which design techniques of mass production have been appropriated by architects when seeking to render operative the interplay between scalar proportions, volumetric outlines, and product articulation. As instances she saw capitalizing on the graphic, Dean examined Aldo Rossi's 1983/1984 "Variations on coffee–makers" (fig. 6.2) and two projects by Greg Lynn, the 1999 Ark of the World Museum San Jose in Costa Rica and his 2003 scheme for Sociópolis in Valencia.[13] For Bob Somol, "Logo" makes graphics performative.[14] Some of the built examples he used included the 2001 Hagen Island housing development by MVRDV, the 2004 Cottbus Library by Herzog & de Meuron, and the 2005 Shipping and Transport College by Neutelings Riedijk (fig. 6.3). Echoing his ongoing interest in questions concerning shape, Somol alluded to tactics such as "intensify an element," "extend the line," "develop a precise but vague silhouette," and "saturate with a monotone treatment" for the conception of logo-buildings. "Icons," as per Jencks's account, do not lend

11. See Penelope Dean, "By No Means Representation," *Hunch, the Berlage Institute Report* 11 (2007): 14–15.

12. See John McMorrough, "Blowing the Lid Off Paint," *Hunch, the Berlage Institute Report* 11 (2007): 64–73.

13. See Penelope Dean, "Blow-Up," *Hunch, the Berlage Institute Report* 11 (2007): 76–83.

14. Robert Somol, "Green Dots 101," *Hunch, the Berlage Institute Report* 11 (2007): 28, 34–35.

6.2 Aldo Rossi. Variations on coffee-makers (1984).

6.3 Neutelings Riedijk. Shipping and Transport College in Rotterdam, The Netherlands (2005); Concert Hall in Bruges, Belgium (2005). Logo-buildings.

themselves to being described in terms of graphic procedures or classifiable actions. Rather, they act through metaphor, and their materialization is all the more successful the more diverse personal interpretations they allow for. Along these lines, in his book *The Iconic Building*, which appeared two years before the issue of *Hunch*, Jencks had introduced the notion of "the enigmatic signifier," which designates a building's "use of precise denotations and fuzzy connotations" in reference to the possibility of insinuating suggestive overtones without falling into either literal figuration or plain abstraction.[15] *The Iconic Building* revolves around the figural associations enabled by the condition of architectural iconicity and focuses on the fundamental determinants of such a condition: the design gestures defining the building's exterior profile (curves, bellies, animal-like contours, loops, abrupt lines, etc.).

While some of these strategies originated earlier in the twentieth century—and it was, therefore, only a different operative instrumentalization that subsequently emerged—the degree to which they have proliferated following the Bilbao Effect is certainly distinctive of our time. Yet, in proliferating while steadily keeping within the purview of the representational break, those strategies have simply been reaffirming the epistemic intensification derived from *Learning from Las Vegas*.

At first glance, a proposition launched by Alejandro Zaera-Polo around 2005 could be read as a challenge to the representational break. The Spanish-born American architect suggested "deliberately associating an image and an organizational system with a coherent entity as a project strategy."[16] He also called for ideas such as "the consistency between the material and the meaningful" and "the development of the discipline of form with a double agenda, that is, operating simultaneously both as an organizational and as a communicative mechanism."[17] On close inspection, however, it turns out the link Zaera-Polo envisioned between representational character and organizational system only hardened the representational break. For one thing, the link was merely

15. Jencks, *The Iconic Building*, 84, 86. Jencks used Daniel Libeskind's proposal for Ground Zero to illustrate this notional construct.

16. Alejandro Zaera-Polo, "La Ola de Hokusai," *Quaderns d'Arquitectura i Urbanisme* 245 (April 2005): 80. My translation and emphasis throughout.

17. Ibid., 86.

established *a posteriori*: it was meant as a tool for communicating projects once they had been finalized, rather than one built into the design process. In this regard, Zaera-Polo spared readers any exhaustive exegesis, himself acknowledging the real purpose of his postulates: "Paradoxically, the most banal and Disneyesque iconography *became the justification*, both conceptual and financial, for the formal experimentation."[18] Second, by "form" and "the material," Zaera-Polo referred only to the building's outside, despite his use of terms such as "organizational system," which seemed to point to the interior.

Consequently, discontinuities between envelope and internal spatial organization ensued, as is evident in the projects that Foreign Office Architects (FOA, Zaera-Polo's firm with Farshid Moussavi) were proposing at the time. For example, the contortions animating their 2002 *Ground Zero* proposal—i.e., the features enabling the scheme to be described in terms of looking like "castellers"—were applied to the masses of the entire buildings (to their shape), whereas internally they housed the usual stack of floor slabs occasionally interrupted by a few sky lobbies.[19] A 2003 tower project for Tenerife, Spain was made to evoke a palm tree, albeit through an outside view alone (fig. 6.4). In their 2004 stadium for the Olympic Park in London, it was the configuration of the outer envelope—segmented in a sequence of curved sections—that became the source of a muscle metaphor. Upon peering into it, however, the stadium was pretty much like any other. The internal spatial disposition of these buildings was not born out of the three-dimensional ethos of the symbolic referent, but rather simply appeared after the fact.[20] Therefore, FOA's work, not unlike the numerous exam-

18. Ibid., 80.

19. The "castellers" are human towers traditionally built during festivals at many locations within Catalonia (Spain).

20. Zaera-Polo's piece, along with two related lectures he had previously delivered at UCLA and Princeton in 2004, prompted some severe criticism. The most penetrating was put forward by Jeff Kipnis, who talked about "literal ways of architectural signification," "the flirtation of FOA with vulgar symbolism," and "withered terms [in reference to the use of 'metaphor']" when referring to the propositions of the Spanish-born American architect. He added that Zaera-Polo had confused "the two referential possibilities of (every) architectural form," namely *the pictorial*—as the realm of representational effects mimicking a reality from a domain other than architecture—and *the significative*—as that which, including the symbolic, alludes to the use of formal and architectural conventions that are historically and traditionally charged with a view to conveying agreed associations and interpretations (e.g. the conventions of classical language). See Jeff Kipnis, "Lo Que Aquí ~~Conseguimos~~ Necesitamos Es ¡No Comunicar!," *Quad-*

6.4 Foreign Office Architects (FOA). Special Plan for Cabo Llanos, Tenerife (2003).

ples offered by Jencks, fell back into the very same representational break, with protocols of signification staying at the level of exterior conditions and problems of dispositional thinking remaining virtually unaddressed.[21]

Organization Through Representation

Kenneth Frampton famously associated two trends that he rooted in the commodification of architectural expression: the reduction of architecture to scenography—which he linked to the triumph of the decorated shed—and the pursuit of spatial invention as an end in itself.[22] Disentangling this conflation,

erns d'Arquitectura i Urbanisme 245 (April 2005): 94–98. My translation. Along the same lines, see Sylvia Lavin, "Conversaciones Acompañadas de Cocktails," *Quaderns d'Arquitectura i Urbanisme* 245 (April 2005): 88–92. Kipnis argued that, in fact, the pictorial, *qua* traditional effect in sculpture, has no equivalent in architecture, where it can only occur as *ornament*—that is, in reference to the part, but never to the whole. Here is where I part from him, for this essay, as shall become more apparent further on, contends the possibility of the exact opposite, namely that ornament can be mobilized in its organizational properties so as to structure the whole of a building. This is precisely the way in which the figural, whether "pictorial" or "significative," bears potential for architecture beyond its effects in the realm of the representational—i.e., insofar as it can enter that of spatial articulation. In the same piece, Kipnis posed the question whether it is possible to conceive of a kind of figuration in architecture that escapes representation, in the sense of eluding the significant effect. While I see my argument as the beginning of an answer to this question, I will not elaborate here on how that is the case. Nor will I discuss how such an argument relates to other aspects that Kipnis associates with the non-significant figural, such as the fact that it is supposed to involve architectural traits that are disciplinary specificities in themselves, and the ways in which these, by avoiding imitation, can only be rooted in the figurative history of the discipline of architecture.

21. The phrase "dispositional thinking" is used here to designate thinking processes in architectural design dealing with questions of three-dimensional spatial disposition. Understanding retrospectively that "The Hokusai Wave" was but a prelude to his subsequent *Politics of the Envelope* project (begun in 2008) would be another way to show that, by the mid-2000s, Zaera-Polo was mostly concerned with questions regarding the external envelope. See Alejandro Zaera-Polo, "The Politics of the Envelope: A Political Critique of Materialism," *Volume* 17 (Fall 2008): 76–106. The ideas he promoted then ought to be seen as the initial manifestations of the increasingly pragmatic element of his thinking. Being preoccupied with getting his projects realized while trying to maintain a certain experimental quality for them, Zaera-Polo started to focus more and more on questions of communication while progressively giving up on the interior. Exemplary of this shift was FOA's John Lewis department store in Leicester (2000–2008), a box-like construction whose skin is a glass façade printed with embroidery patterns. This building is considerably easier to build than, say, a Yokohama Terminal, but it is also not nearly as sophisticated an architectural project. Let us recall that the central premise in *The Politics of the Envelope* was that the architect had largely lost his say in questions of spatial organization, and therefore that he should focus on designing and theorizing the envelope alone.

22. Kenneth Frampton, "Rappel à L'Ordre, the Case for the Tectonic (1990)," in *Theorizing a New Agenda for Architecture, an Anthology of Architectural Theory 1965-1995* (New York, NY: Princeton Architectural Press, 1995), 516–20.

the contention here is that emphasis on the former (i.e., building-as-representation) has come at the expense of attention to the latter (i.e., building-as-spatial-organization). With image architecture operating relentlessly in tune with the duality of these two aspects taken to the extreme—with fancy skins wrapping endless piles of horizontal slabs in towers in Dubai and elsewhere, to offer another example—a dynamic underlying what Sylvia Lavin called "the era of representation" has settled in.[23] Gehry's Guggenheim triggered a widespread appetite in cities across the world to build and own imageable buildings. For one thing, this phenomenon is supported by factors mainly of a socioeconomic and political kind, such as financial profit and representational power. For another, imageable buildings tend to embody an acute exploitation of the duality. Which is to say, contemporary socioeconomic and political factors have come to perpetuate this exploitation, and with these conditions in place, architects design accordingly.

One must question then, whether it is possible to conjure up an alternative to this *status quo* centered around the pervasiveness of the common attributes giving rise to the duck and the decorated shed, since pushing the possibilities of architectural thinking remains a constant demand on the historical development of the discipline. Logically, such an alternative requires a collapse of the duality of building-as-representation versus building-as-spatial-organization, as well as envisioning how this epistemological erasure could operate in the case of imageable architecture. The answer involves conceiving spatial organization through protocols of representation.

Works of architecture envisaged through this approach possess a number of specific characteristics. Their exterior ornamental pattern is part of their internal spatial arrangement. In other words, their identity lies in the synthesis of representational character and spatial disposition; of conditions of imageability and three-dimensional configuration. These conditions do not symbolize or express anything happening on the inside. Rather, they *are* the inside. Thus, distinguishing inside from outside becomes meaningless in an ontological sense—as opposed to rhetorically or merely on perceptual grounds, which has been the case historically in architectural tropes such as "interior and exterior getting mixed up," "both domains flowing into each

23. Lavin, "Practice Makes Perfect," 109.

other," and so forth. The difference with the duck becomes obvious: the duck-envelope symbolizes the function of the building, but its defining qualities have nothing to do with the internal spatial disposition.

Buildings conceived out of this approach may seem to resonate with the outside-as-a-result-of-inside motto of the modern movement, yet by no means do they embody it in the same sense. Modern architects sought to achieve a particular kind of interior-exterior correspondence by treating an independent plane—the façade—so that either program or interior volume (or both) might be legible from the outside. It was about projecting onto the outside wall in order to make it a display of the interior. In contrast, the enclosure of the buildings whose spatial organization has been devised through protocols of representation does not register as an independent element, since whatever is constitutive of their external condition is equally constitutive of their three-dimensional articulation inside.

This essential dissimilarity can also be identified in the process of design thinking leading up to either type of building. In the modernist process, it is usually the interior that makes its way to the exterior, while in the approach advanced here two other procedures may apply. In a reversal of the modernist premise, the inside may be the result of an outside whose representational character is defined at the outset—as in a spatial configuration that develops out of a particular ornamental quality or symbolic profile. Alternatively, the whole structure may be thought of as a three-dimensional arrangement with no predefined volumetric boundaries that dissociate it *a priori* from an external field. In this case, the resulting outside condition is contingent upon the way that such an arrangement manifests itself relative to the specific volumetric envelope that is eventually given—as opposed to it being defined *independently*, or *sequentially afterward* so as to showcase the interior. If in modern architecture the plan was the generator, here it is a particular mode of subdividing space three-dimensionally that provides the originating situation.[24]

After the modern movement's advocacy for the façade as a display of the inside and the intensification of the representational break—faithfully endorsed by Koolhaas's "lobotomy"—the approach put forth here is one whose instantiations are not easy to track down. While there have been ducks and decorated sheds since at least the twelfth century, the first buildings stemming from conceiving spatial organization through protocols of representation comprehensively enough go back only a few decades.[25]

Architect and theorist Alfred Neumann was a pioneer in transferring aspects from the domain of representation—regarding ornament, in particular—to that of spatial disposition. In his 1969 essay "Architecture as Ornament," the father of so-called "architectural morphology" elaborated on the analogies between the structural and ornamental properties of two-dimensional crystallography versus those of its three-dimensional equivalent. He sought to prove the potential of the latter to contribute to the question of spatial arrangement in architecture while maintaining the ornamental order distinctive of a crystallographic aggregation. In a statement condensing such "pattern thinking," Neumann wrote:

> If it is admissible to consider ornament as two-dimensional crystallography, it is equally justified to call crystallography and with it architecture a three-dimensional ornament. For architecture is related to crystallography from the space-packing point of view.[26]

Just as crystallography concerns itself with the regular subdivision of space, space packing deals with the study of specific polyhedra that leave no spaces unaccounted for when placed together in space.[27] The complexity of polyhedra *qua* spatial units is itself the object of space-packing research as well.[28]

24. Elsewhere I have written about one particular species of architecture arising from conceiving spatial organization through protocols of representation: the sponge building. See José Aragüez, "Sponge Territory," *Flat Out 2* (Spring 2017): 32–36, reprinted here on pages 69–79. This species of building displays a series of features particular to it—such as a certain geometric kernel that generates a specific sequence of spaces—while materializing the general principles laid out above.

25. For historical examples of ducks and sheds, see Venturi, Scott Brown, and Izenour, *Learning from Las Vegas*, 104ff.

26. Alfred Neumann, "Architecture as Ornament," *Zodiac* 19 (1969): 90–98.

27. For an elaborate study of the role of space packing in Neumann's architectural thinking, see Rafi Segal, *Space Packed: The Architecture of Alfred Neumann* (Zurich: Park Books, 2018).

28. For an extended definition see Keith Critchlow, "Closepacking," *Zodiac* 22 (1972): 172–78.

It was by placing great emphasis on the problem of the subdivision of space that Neumann set out to recast the nature of space-packed architecture as three-dimensional ornament. Exemplary of this ambition were the Dubiner Apartment House in Ramat-Gan, Israel (1961–63, with Zvi Hecker and Eldar Sharon), and his entry for the Netanya City Hall competition in Netanya, Israel (1964, with Hecker) (fig. 6.5). These buildings were conceived as a grouping of polyhedral cells whose dense aggregational quality, while structuring space, was construed as ornamental.

Neumann displaced architecture's ontological grounds by equating them with those of ornament, and in so doing triggered the possibility of constructing deliberate links between architectural protocols of adornment—typically restricted to two-dimensional elements—and holistic formal arrangements. Yet again, cases like Neumann have been rather uncommon, especially if the same degree of rigor and sophistication is demanded in turning the logic of ornament (or another representational aspect) into that of the spatial arrangement of a fully fledged building. From around the same time, Bertrand Goldberg's Marina City in Chicago (1959–64) stands out conspicuously. The radial character of its spatial organization as well as the disposition of balconies appear linked to the fact that the two towers comprising the complex evoke the metaphor of a flower (fig. 6.6).

From earlier this century, Herzog & de Meuron's Prada Aoyama in Tokyo (2001–2003) is another example. The representational character of this building is determined by the diamond-like pattern on the façade. This pattern is, in fact, a diagrid structure, a few units of which are extruded horizontally at intervals to create singular programmatic areas that cross and articulate the double height spaces they pierce (fig. 6.7). Norman Foster's 30 St. Mary Axe in London (2004) also features a notable consistency between imageability and internal configuration. This building challenges the traditional typology of the floor-upon-floor high rise by establishing a spiral sequence of sky courts that, clustered every six floors, create diagonal perspectives across the interior (fig. 6.8). In terms of representation, the fact that the shape was reduced to a simple yet distinctive volumetric outline made it open to many possible interpretations.[29]

29. See Madelon Vriesendorp's drawings in Jencks, *The Iconic Building*, 186.

6.5 Alfred Neumann with Zvi Hecker. Netanya City Hall Competition in Netanya, Israel (1964).

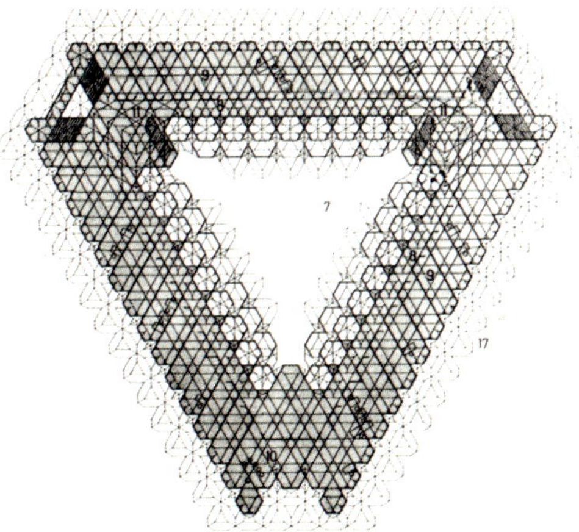

4

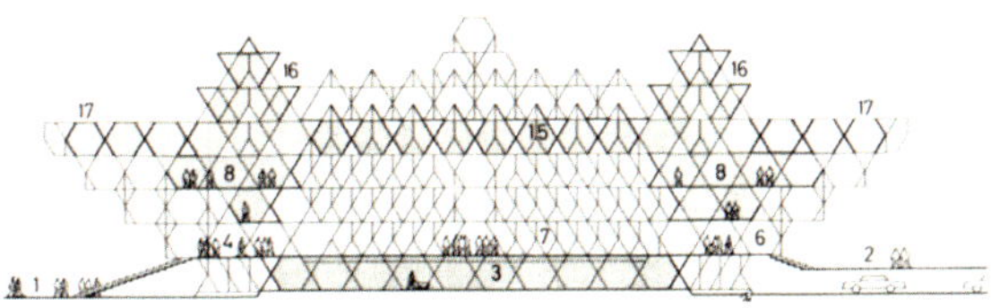

5

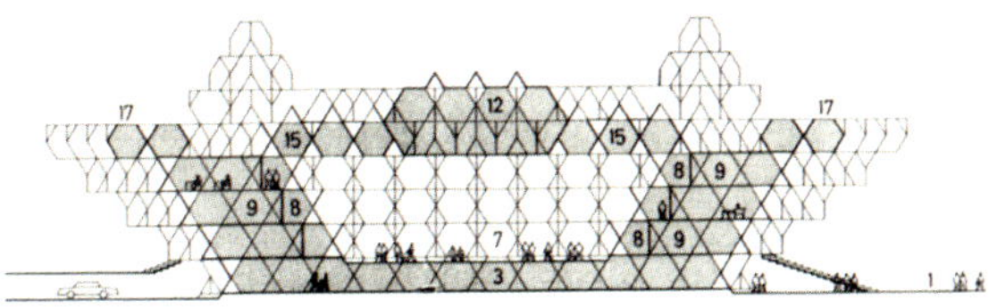

6

4. *Third floor plan;* **5.** *Section through the main and side entrance;* **6.** *Section through the council chamber and offices area. Key to the plans and sections: 1. Lower piazza - 2. Upper piazza (Covering the parking area) - 3. General service and mechanical equipment area - 4. The main entrance from the lower piazza - 5. Side entrance from the parking - 6. Side entrance from the upper piazza - 7. The triangular certral court - 8. Interior galleries - 9. Offices - 10. Major's office - 11. Stairs to the council chamber - 12. Triangular council chamber - 13. Entrance to the council chamber - 14. Roof garden - 15. Truncated*

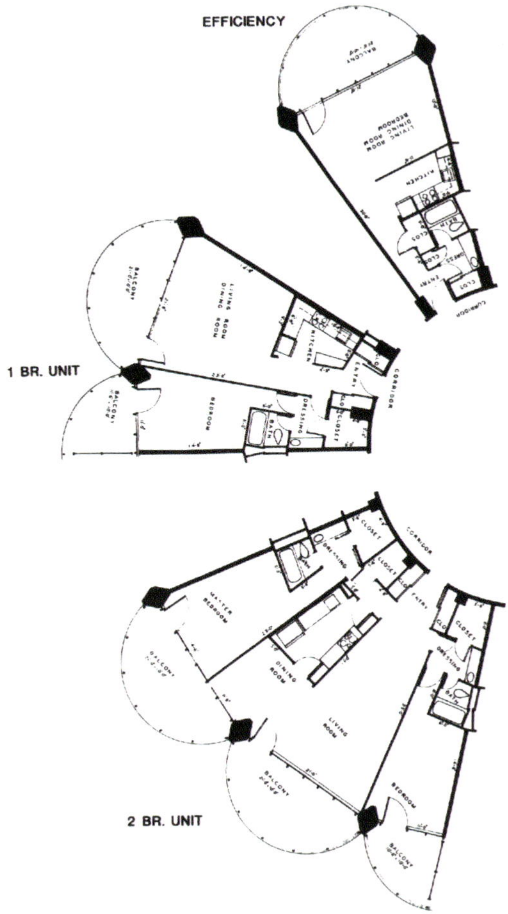

6.6 Bertrand Goldberg. Marina City in Chicago, USA (1959–1964). Typical plan.

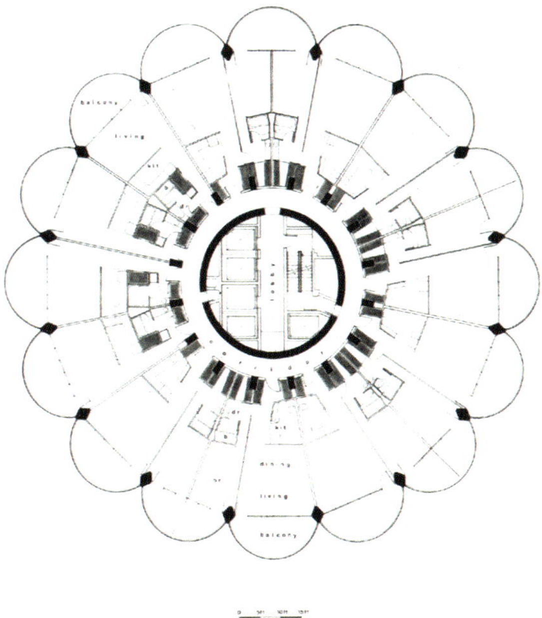
balcony
living
kit
dr
lobby
corridor
dr
b
kit
dining
br
living
balcony

6.7 Herzog & de Meuron. Prada Aoyama in Tokyo, Japan (2001–2003).

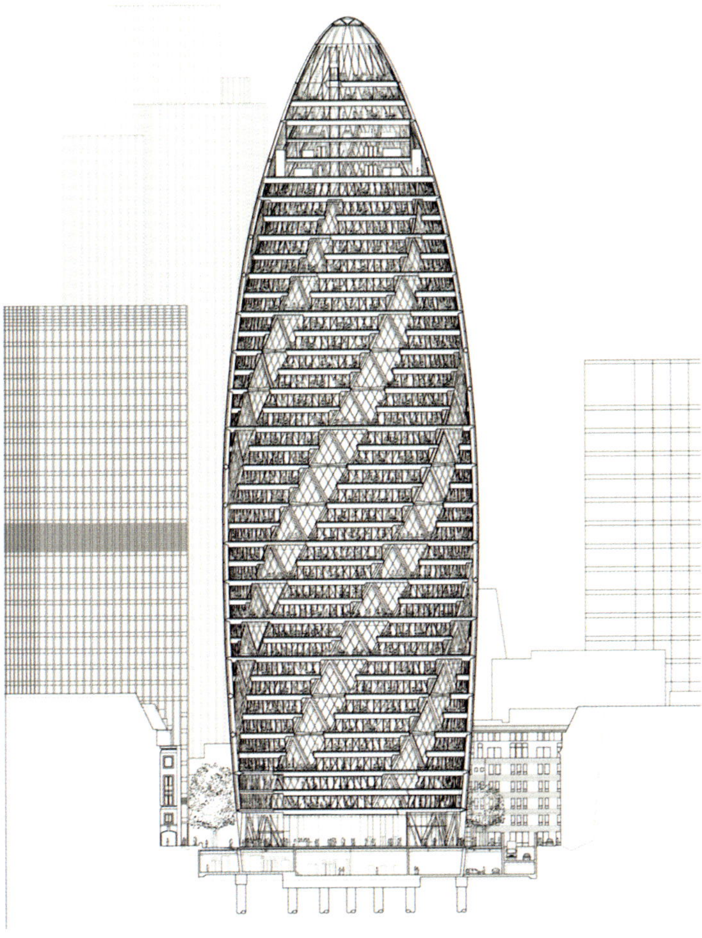

6.8 Foster + Partners. 30 St. Mary's Axe in London, UK (2000–2003).

What is noteworthy here is that both these aspects define one another: 30 St. Mary Axe materializes a distinctive relationship between representational character and spatial disposition, presenting an inextricable bond between its contour being bullet-shaped and the internal spatial arrangement being determined by a succession of spiraling courts. This synthesis is the product of two sets of considerations informing each other: on the one hand, those involving technology, efficiency, and typological subversion; on the other, questions of symbolism and imageability.

More recently, in 2013, Nieto Sobejano completed a Contemporary Art Center in Córdoba whose spatial configuration is analogous to that of the ornamental patterns characteristic of ceilings in traditional Islamic architecture (fig. 6.9). Other relevant instances include Toyo Ito's Taichung Opera House and its predecessor, a 2004 competition entry for the Forum for Music, Dance, and Visual Culture in Ghent, Belgium. The formal arrangement actualized in these buildings stands in direct relationship to the ornamental qualities of sponges.[30]

Toward a Critical Imageability

Though mostly unfolding within the paradigm of the representational break and its intensification, the ways in which design strategies resonating at the level of imageability have been developing over the last twenty-five years bear the imprint of their usage exceeding the sphere of signification alone. For implicit in those strategies is the possibility of their triggering form at a building scale, with this term, "form," construed, not as "shape" or "mass"—that is, concerning merely the sensory properties of a building as they bear on its outline or envelope quality—but rather as a spatial regime of internal organization, disposition, or arrangement. It is precisely through the consistency

30. See Aragüez, "Sponge Territory." The Taichung Opera House is more relevant here than another Ito project brought up more often when questions of representation are at stake: the TOD's Omotesando building in Tokyo, completed in 2004. Here a link only exists between the ornamental qualities of the façade (the fact that it looks like a tree) and its properties as a load-bearing structure, while the rest of the building is a rather conventional floor-upon-floor articulation. For an insightful take on the decorative character of structural envelopes in contemporary architecture, see Nina Rappaport, "Deep Decoration," *30/60/90* 10 (2006): 95–103.

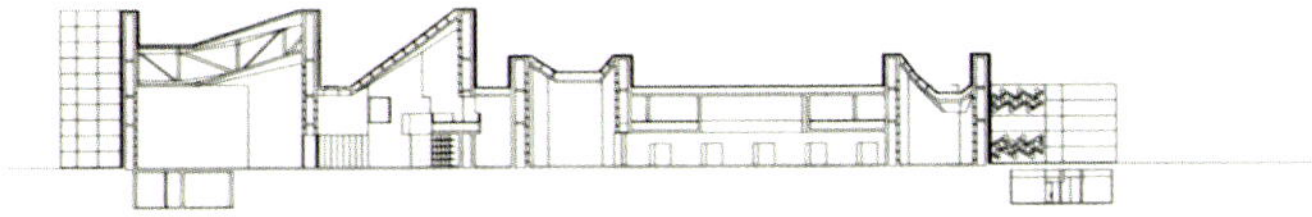

SECTION VIEW OF BLACK BOX

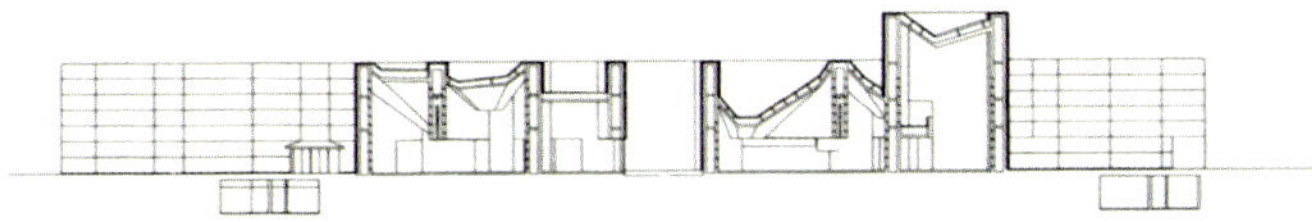

SECTION VIEW OF EXHIBITION AREAS AND PATIOS

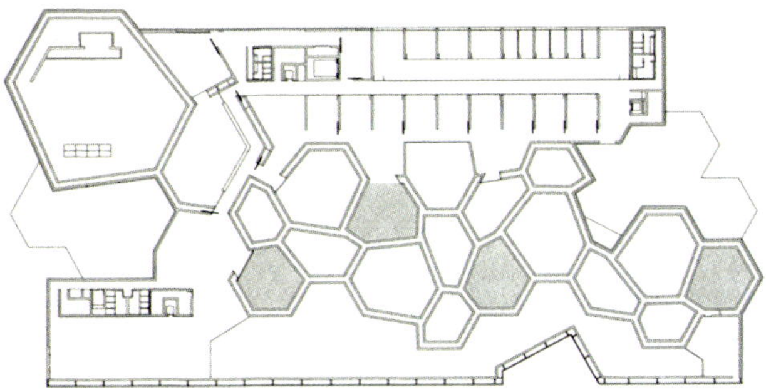

PLAN UPPER LEVEL

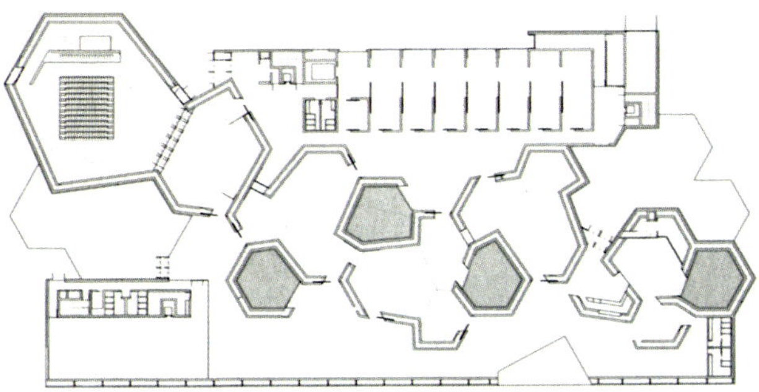

PLAN GROUND LEVEL

6.9 Fuensanta Nieto and Enrique Sobejano. Contemporary Art Center in Córdoba, Spain (2006–2013).

between imageability and form thus understood that such a paradigm at the core of image architecture can be superseded.

In terms of design, the reason to argue for a link between representation and dispositional thinking is fundamentally heuristic, since it unleashes a distinct capacity to prompt novel ways of conceiving spatial arrangements in architecture, as well as the attendant typological and programmatic inventions. In a theoretical sense, the discursive construct around this model gives rise to the realm of *critical imageability*, one that has the capacity to catalyze alternatives to the representational break, and through it to standard spatial arrangements in architecture, commonly dominated by those of a floor-upon-floor nature. The use of criticality invoked here is therefore dialectical rather than resistant; specifically, dialectical with a constructionist element.[31] It is one that mobilizes the very dynamics underwriting the state of affairs—i.e., the twofold, free-floating condition of the architectural image, both in its detachment from formal arrangements and in its capacity to travel across different realms—in order to subvert that very state.

The fact that institutions and agents in power keep capitalizing on architecture's qualities of imageability seems to validate this project, which essentially proposes an attempt to turn the answer to demands on those qualities to the disciplinary advantage of architecture. It has become evident that surrendering to the sociopolitical dynamics driving the desires of the contemporary city is naturally leading to stagnation in terms of the discursive content of architectural design and its history, as it reinforces a paradigm that has been operational for quite some time now. Given this scenario, conceiving spatial

31. The qualifier "constructionist" is used here to invoke a recent tendency in theories of critique within the humanities and social sciences, whereby the final result of criticism is not simply an oppositional, negative view of the current state of affairs, but rather a set of directives toward the construction of a parallel regime of reality. This regime is conceived as the result of reconfigurations and new assemblies of the constituents of the existing reality within the targeted domain, for instance that of perception, signification, and politics, to mention a few. For a discussion of the possibility of a constructionist criticality in architecture at the intersection with this larger tendency in the humanities and social sciences, see José Aragüez, "On Architecture's Metacriticality," in Chris Brisbin and Myra Thiessen, *The Routledge Companion to Criticality in Art, Architecture, and Design* (Milton Park, Abingdon, Oxon; New York, NY: Routledge, 2018), 167–78, reprinted here on pages 81–99. Two texts essential to the larger trend include Jacques Rancière, *The Emancipated Spectator* (London: Verso, 2010), and Bruno Latour, "Why Has Critique Run Out of Steam? From Matters of Fact to Matters of Concern," *Critical Inquiry* 30 (Winter 2004): 225–48.

organization through protocols of representation paves a way out of this stalemate without being oppositional: it tunes in to the specific appeals currently being made on architecture—that is, those on its imageability—yet, in doing so, it critically dismantles the duality underwriting the epistemic intensification brought on by VSBI.

All in all, the position articulated here suggests turning the structures underpinning today's image architecture into something of a critical construct, fostering a particular kind of formal thinking less keen on accidental metaphors than on solid theories of spatial organization based upon protocols of imageability. And it does so by reconciling the two dimensions of building that Frampton considered at odds with one another: "the representational" and "the ontological."[32] For critical imageability rests on the possibility that the former may be instrumentalized in order to make substantial contributions to the realm of the latter (insofar as spatial organization determines the very being of a building; its kernel, its ontological matrix).

By extension, this approach offers an alternative to the current reincarnations of postmodernism, since it targets the representational break that they share with image architecture more generally. In fact, it hints at a larger claim concerning the sidestepping of postmodernism altogether. Namely, postmodernism has typically been characterized along two axes: on the one hand, in relation to theatricality (i.e., historicism and the phenomenon of the building-as-icon); on the other, through questions of interiority (i.e., autonomy, deconstruction, and digital design). Seeking a bond between representational character and spatial disposition entails generating interiority—insofar as such a disposition acquires a logic of its own—*through* theatricality, thereby voiding the divide between the two categories. In other words, the effective hypostatization of protocols of meaning in general—and of ornament, in particular—in their transference from the realm of signification—or, in some cases, from the merely aesthetic—to that of formal organization, constitutes an epistemological shift that can no longer be framed within postmodernist agendas.

32. Frampton, "Rappel à L'Ordre, the Case for the Tectonic (1990)," 516–20.

Spatial Infrastructure

In the culture of architectural thinking, there is a material entity that has escaped detailed reflection as a recognizable ensemble even though it has always existed as a constituent of all buildings. Two different sets of elements jointly determine the way the overall volume of space bounded by a building's external envelope is internally organized. There is, on the one hand, a three-dimensional material set of elements providing the primary articulation of space, prior to the introduction of partitions. This ensemble, which generates a first series of subvolumes of programmed space, is here termed *spatial infrastructure*.[1] The majority of buildings today are articulated around the quintessential spatial infrastructure of the twentieth century, as propounded in Le Corbusier's Maison Dom-Ino: a stack of parallel floor slabs held apart by vertical supports (fig. 7.1).

On the other hand, the second set of elements that contributes to the compartmentalization of interior space is the collection of partition walls. Partitions are subordinate to the spatial infrastructure, since their placement and arrangement can only be decided in relation to it. Further, the spatial infrastructure remains generally unaltered throughout the life of a building, whereas partitions can be changed relatively easily, as needed. In other words, a given spatial infrastructure allows for multiple distributions

1. I first introduced the term "spatial infrastructure" in the context of a studio I taught at Columbia University in spring 2018.

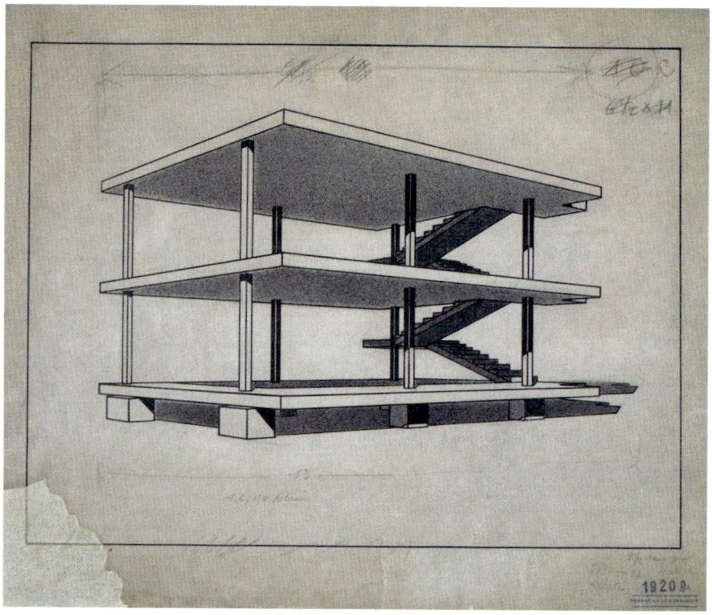

7.1 Le Corbusier, Maison Dom-Ino, 1914.

within an envelope while retaining its three-dimensional specificity. Owing to its hierarchical primacy and degree of permanence, therefore, the spatial infrastructure—and not the partitions—fundamentally defines the internal three-dimensional identity of a building.

Le Corbusier's Maison Dom-Ino triggered a paradigm shift in terms of the distinction between spatial infrastructure and partitions. Up until its generalization, spatial infrastructure and partitions were commonly found to be one and the same.[2] Consider Palladio's Villa Foscari. The spatial infrastructure here comprises a series of floor slabs and right-angled load-bearing walls, but these walls also function as partitions. Or take Borromini's San Carlo alle Quattro Fontane. The entire configurational scheme stems exclusively from the elements embodying the primary internal organization of space, that is, the spatial infrastructure: a series of broken and curved walls to which engaged columns are attached. There are no additional partitions. None of those primary elements can be removed without compromising the building's spatial (and, in this case, structural) integrity. Le Corbusier's Dom-Ino of 1914 inaugurated a new norm. Partitions became a separate set of elements relative to those establishing the primary internal articulation of space, columns, and slabs. As a result, in modern and contemporary architecture—though spatial infrastructure and partitions might still occasionally be merged—the two sets of elements are usually discernible on the basis of hierarchy and permanence.

Insofar as it relates to architectural thinking, the realm of spatial infrastructure stays within the confines of the architectural scale.[3] As is well known, the term "infrastructure" appears frequently in the disciplines concerned

2. It is the dominant tendency—in Western architecture specifically, but also, in many cases, beyond—that is being referred to here. Counterexamples include certain bents of traditional Japanese architecture and medieval timber frame structures.

3. Architectural thinking refers here to the repository of discursive knowledge engendered through the analysis, discussion, and conceptualization of aspects of two inextricably imbricated regimes: that of the building and that of the design process leading up to it. In this proposition, the term *discursive* is utilized in its classical sense, which alludes to the kind of knowledge that involves premises, narratives, concepts, ideas, judgments, inferences, conclusions, etc. as channeled through thought and expressed through language. Architectural thinking distinguishes itself from other domains pertaining to design, such as product, furniture, exhibition, or installation design, urbanism, etc., each of which revolves around a distinct object of knowledge ascertainable through its set of specificities. Architectural thinking is therefore a specific domain of knowledge—if a nonautonomous one, as it is connected to any number of other domains and to culture at large.

with the built environment, where it also has spatial implications—albeit of a different nature. In civil engineering, "infrastructure" tends to designate roads, bridges, dams, and works of similar magnitude and purpose. In reference to the city, it alludes variously to power grids and sewage systems, as well as to buildings and public spaces as notable presences within a larger urban construct, whether they be seen physically, programmatically, or institutionally. In architecture, as distinguishable from both civil engineering and urbanism, spatial infrastructure limits itself to that which takes place within a building's envelope.

The qualifier "spatial" in relation to infrastructure emphasizes the fact that the material ensemble it characterizes possesses a marked level of intricate and expanded three-dimensionality, in contrast to a mostly planar or bidimensional unfolding.[4] Through this three-dimensionality, a spatial infrastructure gives rise to a series of qualitatively identifiable sectors within a bounded volume of space. Thus, the relationship between space and infrastructure is one in which the former is taken as the stuff awaiting ordering—as a homogenous amalgam brought to a first stage of organization by the components of the infrastructure. This incipient stage of organization entails certain proportions and relational properties, such as those governing the arrangement of horizontal surfaces in height, the disposition of the vertical elements relative to those surfaces, and the way various spatial sectors present themselves three-dimensionally.

Beyond a descriptive label designating a material ensemble that has always existed in buildings, the term spatial infrastructure is here turned into a concept. The conceptual purpose of spatial infrastructure is two-fold: on the one hand, as an analytical category; on the other, as a design tool capable of projecting architectural thinking forward. As an analytical category, spatial infrastructure shifts our perspective on architecture, enabling an understan-

4. With the exception of a building's load-bearing structure—an engineering form to be sure, but one featuring a distinctive internal three-dimensionality determined by architecture's inhabitability—engineering forms such as roads, dams, shells, and roof structures lack the same degree of intricacy in their unfolding, even when they do so three-dimensionally. Frei Otto's membranes and Heinz Isler's sheds come to mind as relevant examples: their organizational intricacy is practically negligible even when compared to that embodied in a simple single-family house. Fundamental differences in degree and kind of organizational intricacy distinguish architectural form from engineering form.

ding of both the history of the field and contemporary production through a different lens. Indeed, a new series of paradigms for thinking about buildings can be uncovered when using the concept analytically—for example, the paradigms around the Dom-Ino scheme: pre-Dom-Ino, Dom-Ino-based, and beyond Dom-Ino. Further, since the spatial infrastructure as such is seldom the focal point in an architectural design scenario (the external envelope, contextual gestures, the massing of a program, or particular materials are more common entry points into the design of a building), the concept can be expanded to give rise to a novel design framework: *the spatial infrastructure approach.*

Against the pervasiveness of Dom-Ino, alternatives started to emerge somewhat more frequently around the mid-twentieth century, albeit still few and far between. Think of Frederick Kiesler's variations of his Endless House and some of Alfred Neumann's experiments with polyhedric architecture, both dating from the 1950s and 1960s. Whether through folding surfaces in the former's case or polyhedral aggregations in the latter's, the spatial infrastructures materialized in those designs are not reducible to the Dom-Ino prototype.[5]

The paradigms around the Dom-Ino scheme are some of the central ones unearthed out of an analytical use of the concept of spatial infrastructure. Concerning the use of the concept as a design tool vis-à-vis such paradigms, the spatial infrastructure approach contributes one specific route to the generation of alternatives to the Dom-Ino scheme—alternatives which, to this day, remain a minority in relation to the dominance of Dom-Ino-based architecture and its derivatives.[6]

5. Cedric Price's Fun Palace from the early 1960s could also be cited here. The spatial infrastructure of this building (not to be mistaken for its structural bar-and-node trusses and vertical supports) is composed of a number of programmatic enclosures and platforms which are three-dimensionally scattered within a larger volume. The disposition of these enclosures and platforms in space cannot be easily derived from the seriality of the Dom-Ino scheme. However, unlike Kiesler and Neumann, Price's pervasive use of the box theme kept the Fun Palace firmly tied to modernist architecture.

6. Two buildings may feature, say, cantilevers in different positions, diverse colors here and there, light wells and courtyards laid out in dissimilar configurations; one may be rather tall, the other low-rise. But if they share the same essential spatial infrastructure comprising a stack of horizontal floor slabs held up by vertical linear supports, then both will be derivative of the Dom-Ino scheme.

While a spatial infrastructure exhibits a distinct potential for human occupancy (which is by no means a property of every conceivable three-dimensional organization), it does not yet constitute a building. A building results from the realization of that potential into a fully fledged navigation device that houses a particular program—a device including partitions, façades, all-around accessibility, intelligibility of spatial sequences, climatic and environmental conditioning, etc. A spatial infrastructure can therefore be viewed as a building *in embryo*: it embodies the spatial kernel of a building, although it still requires many additional elements to become a wholly developed work of architecture. For example, the spatial kernel of Herzog & de Meuron's Prada Aoyama—i.e., its spatial infrastructure—comprises a series of floor slabs, three prominent vertical cores, and a few horizontal extrusions providing programmatic areas that cross and articulate the double-height spaces they pierce. These extrusions stem from a diamond pattern on the façade, which at the same time functions as a diagrid structure. Remarkably, this is one of the few instances in the history of architecture where a two-dimensional motif on a building envelope triggers the main elements of its internal spatial organization.[7]

Since a spatial infrastructure, insofar as it is architectural, is ultimately meant to be occupied by a collection of human or human-related activities, it is required that it be built. Therefore, when considering spatial infrastructure in a medium other than the erection of the built artifact itself, it must be presupposed that it could be built, this *buildability* inflecting its conception in a particular way. At this juncture it may seem that the concept of spatial infrastructure is very close to Kenneth Frampton's "structural unit as the irreducible essence of architectural form," which in turn echoes Karl Bötticher's notion of *Kernform*.[8] Indeed, spatial infrastructure and Frampton's "structural unit" are related, but they are not the same. First, Frampton's formulation designates the structural framework *per se*—as an assemblage of constructional elements—whereas the thrust of spatial infrastructure lies

7. The Basilica of Sant'Andrea in Mantua can be considered a precedent, albeit a distant one, since the correspondence between envelope and internal organization in Alberti's building is not as literal and comprehensive as found in the reduced lineage to which Prada Aoyama belongs.

8. See Kenneth Frampton, "Rappel à L'Ordre, the Case for the Tectonic (1990)," in *Theorizing a New Agenda for Architecture, an Anthology of Architectural Theory 1965-1995* (New York, NY: Princeton Architectural Press, 1995), 516–28.

in the organization of space it begets. Second, spatial infrastructure does not prioritize "the tectonic," unlike Frampton's structural unit. Third, the primary load-bearing framework plays an essential role in the materialization of a spatial infrastructure, but is not *a priori* coextensive with it. This distinction is not clear in Pezo von Ellrichshausen's related notion of "spatial structure," even though the very word "structure" partakes in the term. In fact, just exactly in what register spatial structure falls is not clear to begin with. Unlike spatial infrastructure, which is a material ensemble, spatial structure seems to be primarily an abstract, representational construct, since Pezo von Ellrichshausen refers to it variously as a "system of relations" and a "mental image."[9]

To be sure, sometimes load-bearing framework and spatial infrastructure are one and the same. At Mansilla + Tuñón's Castilla and León Museum of Contemporary Art in León, Spain, selected vertical extrusions within a pattern of adjacent stripes made up of alternating squares and rhombi provide the main spatial organization for the building and constitute the load-bearing walls (fig. 7.2). Yet structure and spatial infrastructure do not always necessarily coincide. At FOA's Yokohama Terminal, for example, the material construct engendering the building's spatial organization is a continuous, nondirectional surface—encompassing bifurcating paths, flat open areas, and smooth transitions between levels—which is not itself the primary load-bearing structure. Rather, this surface is held in place by a discrete, bi-directional assemblage of transversal ribs and longitudinal girders (fig. 7.3).

A given spatial infrastructure transcends the particularities of the final building into which it evolves, whether in terms of materials, program, dimensions, volumetric contours, or any combination of these attributes. In other words, the same spatial infrastructure is capable of extensive differentiation: scalable and deployable in diverse contexts, it can be made into various dissimilar buildings, though it will not lose its defining identity. A spatial infrastructure is distinct by virtue of its specificities, while its degree of abstraction—relative to a fully fledged building—makes it generalizable. Consider, for instance, the spatial infrastructure made up of a spiraling sequence of programmatic sloping planes, shifting in dimension and shape, that unfolds

9. See Pezo von Ellrichshausen, *Spatial Structure* (Copenhagen, Denmark: Arkitektur B, 2016), 139–40, 218–19.

7.2 Mansilla+Tuñón Architects. MUSAC in León, Spain (2001–2004). Interior view: Galleries. Walls both organize space and serve as load-bearing structure.

from the bottom to the top of the building while intersecting a regular grid of columns that equally takes up the entirety of the interior volume. This same spatial infrastructure is found both in OMA's Jussieu libraries (fig. 7.4) and MVRDV's Villa VPRO, two buildings with vastly different programs envisaged for vastly different sites.

Shifting attention from the building as a whole—or any one of its elements—to its spatial infrastructure opens up a particularly productive design territory, along the following lines. Though capable of realistically housing a set of human activities, a spatial infrastructure precedes programmatic specialization. Due to its embryonic state, it may ultimately be occupied by a number of different programs. Think back to the example of the stacked horizontal floors: this spatial infrastructure can be appropriated for either a hotel, an office tower, or a branch library. Therefore, the design territory prompted by the spatial infrastructure approach rests on the suspension of any direct correspondence of form to program and a simultaneous retention of a fundamental, viable programmatic capability for the three-dimensional organization being devised. Evidently, it is vital that a final building completed out of a given spatial infrastructure successfully address the requirements of its design scenario. Yet, devoting increased attention to the genesis of material organizations capable of housing different programs directly tackles the growing necessity for works of architecture to accommodate alterations relating to occupancy changes over time.

The importance of the concept of spatial infrastructure also lies in the fact that the emphasis it places on spatial organization is conducive to making substantial contributions to this central domain of architecture. Any spatial infrastructure embodying a previously unavailable three-dimensional organization extends the bounds of possibility of their conception and realization, and with it those of architectural thinking at large. This is the main *raison d'être* of spatial infrastructure: to serve as a heuristic device for creating new models of spatial organization in architecture. To this effect, the ten points below elaborate on spatial infrastructure as a concept leading to a design approach, and articulate a number of additional notions, arguments, and theoretical propositions that are necessary to both support such an approach and further work out the epistemological texture of the concept.

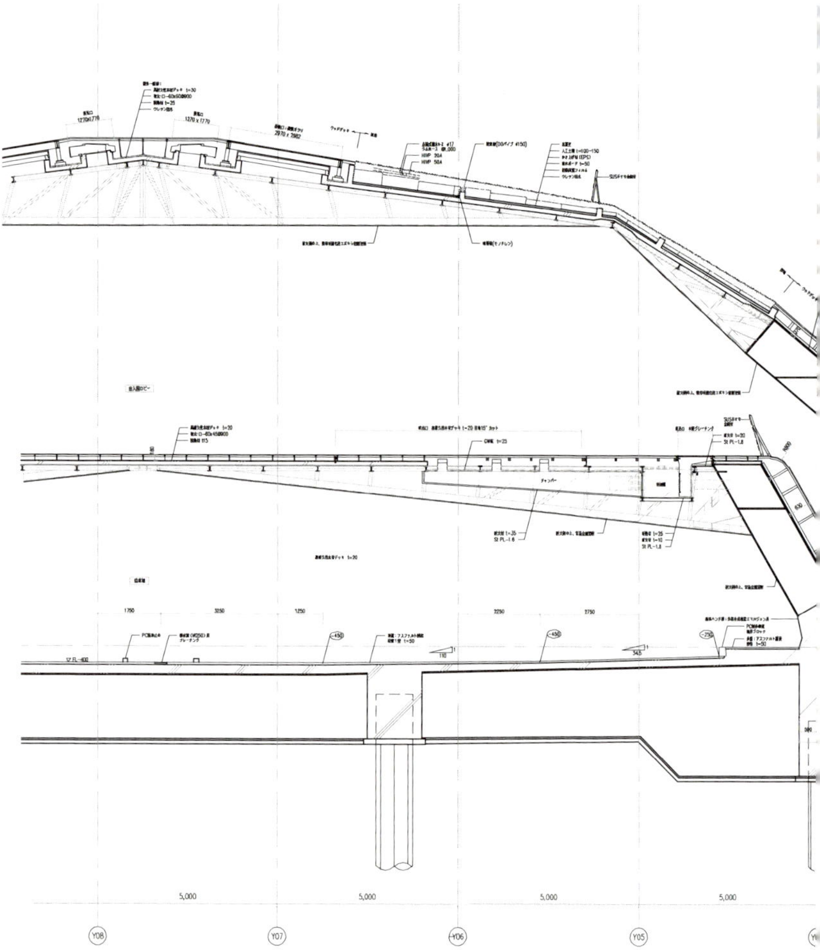

7.3 Foreign Office Architects (FOA). Yokohama International Passenger Terminal in Yokohama, Japan (1995–2002). Transversal section, detail of design stage. Ribs and longitudinal girders hold the building's topographic surface in place.

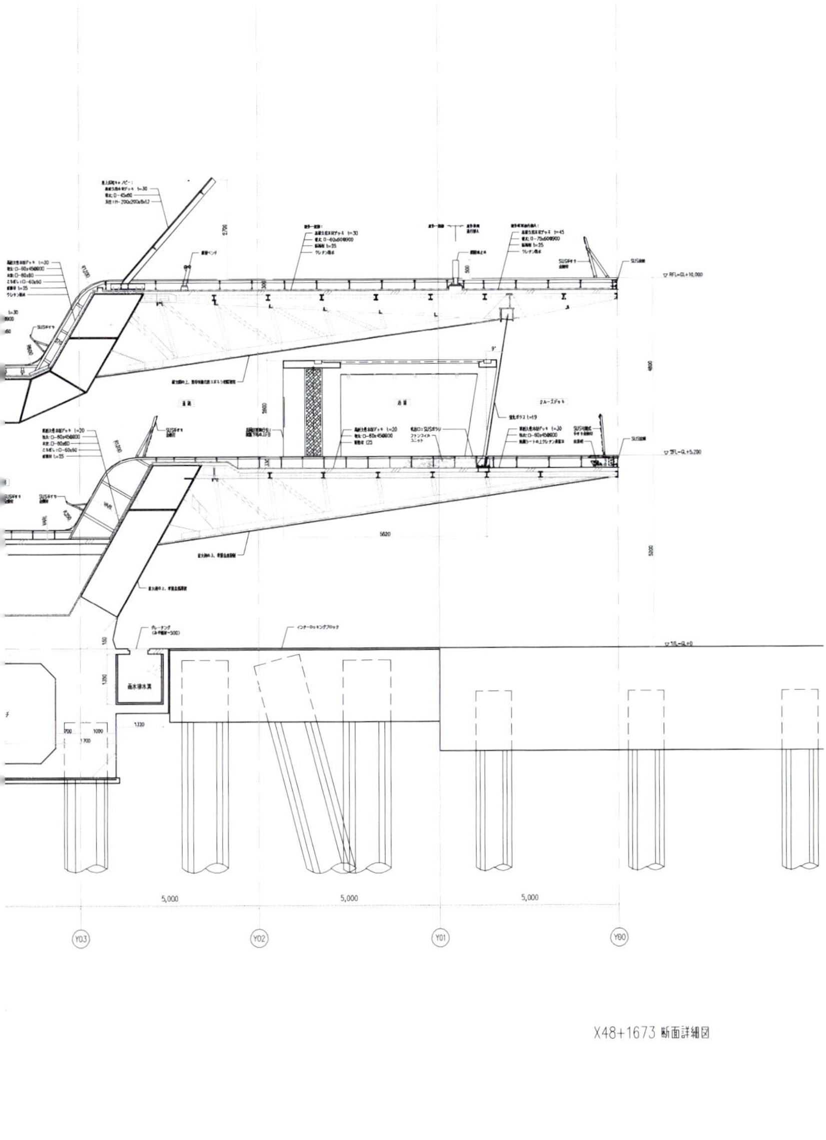

X48+1673 断面詳細図

7.4 OMA/Rem Koolhaas. Competition entry for two libraries in Jussieu, Paris, France (1992). Model.

1. Form vs. Shape

Spatial infrastructure is partly to be framed in regard to historical discussions around the question of form. Within that tradition, proposing spatial infrastructure as a primary regime of architectural thinking requires a shift from the current focus on shape—that which concerns an external envelope, volumetric outline, mass, and other figural conditions—to an emphasis on form as a construct grounded in spatial organization. More precisely, form involves organization in a two-fold sense. On the one hand, it comprises the material elements deployed three-dimensionally whose ensemble makes up the spatial infrastructure. Form, therefore, *embodies* the very organization of those elements. On the other hand, that three-dimensional ensemble gives rise to a sequence of spaces ordered in a manner linked to—but not coincidental with—its material elements. Form *begets* a specific organization of space.

2. Programmatic Immanence

A spatial infrastructure must be endowed with a capacity to house a considerable range of human or human-related activities: a "considerable range" because it precedes programmatic specialization; "human or human-related activities" because housing a number of those is the purpose of the building it will eventually become. This is to suggest that a programmatic potential ought to be immanent to any spatial infrastructure insofar as it is architectural, and therefore that *inhabitability* is a condition of spatial infrastructure.[10] From the first two points combined, it follows that spatial infrastructure synthesizes two principal denominators: on the one hand, the organizational aspect of form; on the other, program as its inherent content, as opposed to an *a posteriori* infill. As a programmatically inflected three-dimensional organization, spatial infrastructure distinguishes itself from the outcomes of the merely morphological operations to which digital practices have largely limited themselves since the 1990s.

10. It is worth comparing this set of propositions to those Andrew Benjamin offered in 2000 regarding what he termed variously the "interarticulation," "indissolubility," and "homology" between function or program, on the one hand, and form, design, or architecture, on the other. Having diverse goals, his epistemological framework differs greatly from the one proposed here. See Andrew Benjamin, *Architectural Philosophy* (University of London, UK: The Athlone Press, 2000), 2–4, 9–10, 72, 74–75.

3. Purposeful Equilibrium Between Order and Differentiation: Toward Three-Dimensional Field Conditions

Because spatial infrastructure designates first and foremost an organizational ensemble, its conceptual working-through vis-à-vis design must grapple with the most advanced theoretical framework put forward in recent times concerning the organizational domain of architectural thinking: Stan Allen's *field conditions*. The spatial infrastructure approach delivers new organizational schemes through a series of patterns, underlying rules, and/or codifiable design gestures. These serve a double purpose: on the one hand, they channel the kind of ascertainable singularity that enables a meaningfully legible expansion of the domain of spatial organization in architecture; on the other, they are to be conceived so that the emerging organizational scheme can productively incorporate chance, variations, and obstacles by means of localized adjustments. By standing at the edge of control—being coherent and yet diverse, consistent and yet nuanced—a spatial infrastructure can respond and mutate in relation to the urban context in which it is ultimately situated. Like field conditions, therefore, spatial infrastructure favors a deliberate equilibrium between order—whether latent or apparent—and differentiation. The chief contribution with respect to Allen's propositions is that, while field conditions tend to unfold primarily in two dimensions (the third dimension appearing typically as a mere vertical extrusion), the spatial infrastructure approach aims for a deployment of such conditions in three dimensions. To that end this deployment ought to unfold along two axes: first, concerning the ways in which the individual connectivity of elements (i.e., part-to-part relationships or "local syntax") can generate a system;[11] and second, in terms of the openness of that system determining, among other things, its ability to integrate extensions and distortions in size, accommodate extraneous entities and other sorts of accidents, and have elementary units added or subtracted to allow for programmatic protrusions and voids within.

4. Critical Process

The study of any spatial infrastructure cannot be disengaged from the form-thinking and form-making leading to it, since discussions of design

11. See Stan Allen, "From Object to Field: Field Conditions in Architecture and Urbanism," *Architectural Design* 67 (June 1997): 25.

process and outcome in architecture need to be inextricably bound together. Within this general precept, spatial infrastructure attempts a critical dialecticization of the process-outcome pairing, dissociating the two terms from each other while keeping them in tension. Following the previous point, the spatial infrastructure approach gives rise to design processes grounded at once in the generative role of the local condition and a holistic openness. This double condition lends the design process a distinctive combination of intelligibility and flexibility. Indeed, the logic underwriting the process will be traceable to an individuated element or action, while the outcome will remain flexible enough as it emerges to incorporate differentiation within. Insofar as a design process of this kind is meant to produce wholes of a specific nature—coherent yet differentiated—it ultimately establishes the framework according to which its outcomes are to be assessed. In other words, the design process itself here becomes a critical tool. The outcome will be successful to the extent it embodies a delicate balance between variation and repetition, diversity and consistency, indeterminacy and order, chance and laws, the individual and the collective, figure and field.

5. Beyond Separation Between Floors

An intense concentration on spatial infrastructure can be a means to freeing buildings from their habitual identification with the uniformly stratified space of the Maison Dom-Ino. Rather than some version of a vertical pile of slabs, the spatial infrastructure approach is attuned to overcoming clear-cut separations between levels through an array of distinct configurational properties. Such properties introduce alternative ways of organizing the various spatial regions for program as well as novel relationships between the itineraries running around and through them. As a determinant of these possibilities, the three-dimensionality of the organizational schemes produced through the spatial infrastructure approach is best captured in perspectival and axonometric representations, with plans, sections, and 2D diagrams supplying partially informative X-rays.

6. Distinctive Spatial Qualities

The new spatial infrastructures pursued here allow for multiple distributions within—partitions and structure being independent—while materializing a specific configuration which, far from being neutral, possesses a number of singular spatial attributes. Through these attributes a spatial infrastructure can resist any compromise on architectural qualities in the name of flexibility. In other words, the distinctive qualities of a spatial infrastructure stem directly from the internal organization it embodies and are to be opposed to the mere wrapping character of a container of space. Thus, the spatial infrastructure approach distances itself from the kind of conventional interpretation of the term "infrastructure" that has historically endorsed more or less neutral, shed-like spaces along with the machine-like aesthetics often characterizing their enclosure. The Pompidou Center is a case in point. Otherwise an invaluable contribution to the history of architecture, the building is fundamentally a pile of parallel slabs giving rise to a sequence of empty, generic spaces. Another relevant, earlier example is Peter Behrens' AEG Turbine Factory, whose technological envelope simply wraps a single big space. In contrast, a noteworthy example is the spatial infrastructure found in Toyo Ito and Andrea Branzi's 2004 runner-up competition entry for the Forum for Music, Dance and Visual Culture in Ghent (Belgium). Here two complementary subspaces define each other as they unfold in three dimensions by means of sequential interpenetrations, without ever intersecting. They remain independent all across the building and yet form a series of interweaving regions that are adjacent to each other throughout, a so-called "sponge surface" serving as a separating membrane in between. Only if this membrane is perforated can a direct connection between the two sets of spaces occur. These series of conditions can be captured by the notion of *spatial reciprocity*, the potential of which has barely been explored despite its obvious architectural resonances. Indeed, architectural design often operates on the basis of heuristic binaries, such as public versus private and open versus compartmentalized, that lend themselves to being articulated through reciprocal spaces in a particularly productive manner.[12]

7. Soft Zoning

The epistemological framework proposed here intimates that the organizational nature of a work of architecture is traceable to its spatial infrastructure as a three-dimensional ensemble preceding the definition of wall partitions. At the same time—aiming to devise experimental alternatives in terms of this organizational nature—the spatial infrastructure approach brings about

12. I first introduced the term *spatial reciprocity* in José Aragüez, "Sponge Territory," *Flat Out* 2 (Spring 2017): 32, reprinted here on pages 69–79.

a certain three-dimensional elaborateness. Implicitly, these two considerations combined play down the idea of "room" and direct attention toward the multiple distributional possibilities embedded in that three-dimensional elaborateness. For, rather than prompting a specific compartmentalization unequivocally, new spatial infrastructures can accommodate a range of possible interior arrangements among which only one is actualized at any one time based on how the various areas are merged or separated, organized, and dimensioned. Compartmentalization strategies based upon hard dividing lines that fix a particular partition scheme undercut that multiplicity, which instead favors what can be termed *soft zoning*. In contrast to building elements that clearly differentiate themselves from the surrounding field (such as walls), the main programmatic areas in a soft zoning regime are dependent on thresholds, that is, spaces that can sometimes themselves house program in addition to their connective role. These thresholds and main programmatic areas come closer to the character of regions than rooms: their identity is recognizable, but their limits can fluctuate. Soft zoning exploits the potential of spatial infrastructures to be occupied differently over time by avoiding the limitations that tend to come with the rigidity of pervasive partitioning. In so doing, it induces a degree of activity hybridization which, if desirable and pursued, can ultimately lead to the reconfiguration of received programmatic packages. Essentially, the soft zoning approach decodifies the ways in which a programmatic tissue inheres in a given spatial infrastructure by unveiling the dispositional and enclosure strategies intrinsic to its attributes.

8. From Architecture vs. Engineering to *Architecture-Engineering Hybrid*

Given the buildability of spatial infrastructure and the central role played by the load-bearing structure in its materialization, the necessity to consider engineering in the development of its conceptual realm emerges as a matter of course. The current proliferation of a novel type of scientifically driven designer in architecture signals that the limits of the engineering mindset, traditionally rooted in science, are stretching, and consequently, that the distinction between architecture and engineering is blurring. Certain engineering inclinations central to what can be called *the architecture-engineering hybrid*—a design attitude at the intersection of both disciplines—are especially productive for engendering new spatial infrastructures.[13] The central role of math and geometry, a marked physical empiricism, the importance of procedural thinking, the interpretation of the organizational laws of nature in terms of design, a focused intensity devoted to the artifact itself (as opposed to its surroundings)—these engineering inclinations are distinguished by their attunement to yielding architectural outcomes. At the same time, they facilitate the kinds of patterns, rules, and codifiable gestures that spawn the characteristic singularity of models of spatial organization in architecture featuring true newness. Even if the structural engineering of a work of architecture may occasionally be incorporated from the early design stages, that does not necessarily mean that the architecture-engineering hybrid as understood here is in operation. For this hybrid entails a specific sort of subversive disciplinarity based upon a *two-fold structural awareness*; one that synthesizes, on the one hand, "structure" in the traditional sense of the building's physical support (load-bearing structure) and, on the other, the organizational traits of spatial infrastructure. This two-fold structural awareness enables properties of the former aspect to be abstracted and turned into a generative spatial code in the latter. Through it, the spatial infrastructure approach prompts a shift from the most common case of structure as a series of neutral elements, unrelated to the conception of the building (architecture vs. engineering), to *structure as a spatial medium* coextensive with the said conception (architecture-engineering hybrid).[14]

9. From Concealment to Integration of Services

Louis Kahn famously discriminated between "served" and "servant" spaces, with the latter encompassing mechanical engineering requirements (ducts, pipes, etc.) as well as connective elements such as stairs, elevators, and corridors. Rather than placing the servant spaces in the building's leftover areas or subordinating them to the served spaces, the spatial infrastructure approach

13. The term "architecture-engineering hybrid" relates to Antoine Picon's "hybrid architect engineer." See Antoine Picon, *Marc Mimram: Hybride Architecte Ingénieur = Hybrid Architect Engineer* (Gollion, Switzerland: In folio, 2007). While Picon referred to the figure of one hybrid architect-engineer, here a different term is used in order to articulate a design attitude more generally and expand on its implications at an epistemological level.

14. In a sense, this can be viewed as a return to a pre-modern attitude to building, albeit with the contemporary tools now at our disposal—both in architectural thinking and technology—and within the specific framework laid out in this point.

explores ways in which the hierarchy between the two kinds of space can be productively dissolved. After Toyo Ito's fundamental breakthrough at the Sendai Mediatheque—involving the use of porous yet concentrated structural clusters to wrap vertical systems and circulation (fig. 7.5)—the spatial infrastructure approach poses the question anew as to whether servant spaces might not only be envisioned in connection with the structure, but might also at times become the very elements articulating a building.[15] Indeed, the specificities of a spatial infrastructure's three-dimensional fabric may naturally dictate the deployment of services and flows within, thereby channeling a rethinking of the relationship between them.

10. Stylistic Nonreferentiality

The aesthetic elements comprising a style typically include decoration, ornament, color palettes, textures, materials, embellishments, and more generally, surface components and details of various kinds. These elements unfold primarily at the level of volumetric envelope and figural conditions, that is, at the level of shape rather than form. A given spatial infrastructure is stylistically nonreferential, since it transcends a building's aesthetic definition. Indeed, the determination of a spatial infrastructure's fundamental make-up can only be traced to the organizational aspect of form, irrespective of how it is aesthetically rendered. Accordingly, a design framework around spatial infrastructure can be constructed without any direct link to a predetermined architectural vocabulary, set of aesthetic codes, or specific representational references. The paradox here is that, while style is inconsequential to spatial organization, extending the bounds of spatial organization may nevertheless afford significant contributions to the aesthetic repository of architecture. As is the case with other projects by Ito—like the Ghent scheme mentioned above and the Taichung Opera House—spatial infrastructures featuring a high degree of singularity are capable of catalyzing contributions to the subdomain of shape to which aesthetic expression belongs. For such singularity prevents the resulting building from being describable on the basis of any received stylistic framework, and this outsideness enables an expansion of the expressive imaginary of architecture. Further, since the spatial infra-

15. For more on Ito's Sendai Mediatheque as relevant to this point, see Juan Antonio Cortés, "Sendai Mediatheque: Three Critical Levels," in José Aragüez, ed., *The Building* (Zürich, Switzerland: Lars Müller Publishers, 2016), 276–85.

structure approach is grounded in stylistic nonreferentiality and its tenets can be satisfied through many possible organizational strategies, it follows that such tenets are able to facilitate the conception of vastly dissimilar buildings. Consequently, whenever consistency is desired across a body of work, the spatial infrastructure approach offers an alternative to the characteristic repetition that results from allegiance to a particular style.

7.5 Toyo Ito. Sendai Mediatheque in Sendai, Japan (1995–2000).

Pattenting Arrangement

Structural engineering involves an operational use of aspects pertaining to science and a scientific frame of mind to devise and craft form. In other words, engineering revolves around the scientization of form. The central role of math, geometry, and physics; a focused intensity devoted to the artifact itself, and less so to context in the wider sense; an interpretation of nature as a source of patterns and configurational laws, rather than as one of mimicry; a profuse enactment of logical, procedural thinking; a lesser emphasis on the experiential dimension in comparison to architecture—the most characteristic engineering inclinations are and have traditionally been connected with its scientific character. Indeed, a rational, scientific strain in engineering skills, which was becoming increasingly pronounced, was central to the split between architecture and engineering at the end of the eighteenth century.

One field that paints a meaningful picture of the evolution of this scientization of form in engineering is that of patents. Painfully under-researched in the histories of both engineering and architecture,[1] the bodies of patent pro-

1. In terms of architectural patents, two of the few recent references out there in English are Mark Garcia, "Architectural Patents and Open-Source Architectures: The Globalization of Spatial Design Innovations (or Learning from 'E99')," in *Architectural Design* 86, no. 5 (September 2016): 92–99, and Martina Decker, "Novelty and Ownership: Intellectual Property in Architecture and Design," in *Technology | Architecture + Design* 1, no. 1, (2017): 41–47. Regarding a host of different subjects around civil and structural engineering patents, such as

duction released over the last two centuries thoroughly reflect the multiple phases of progress that have followed one another. Extremely broad in reach, patent laws vary from continent to continent and from country to country, but a central criterion of patentability is shared. It requires novelty relative to so-called "prior art," that is previously publicly available information concerning the subject matter to be patented. The European Patent Office specifically calls for an "inventive step" and for the invention's susceptibility to "industrial application."[2] The United States Patent and Trademark Office demands "nonobviousness," that is, that the invention not be obvious to a person of regular skills in the field where the invention is claimed.[3] Certain kinds of patents are granted on the basis of the utility of the invention; others, on the aesthetic appearance and ornamental features thereof. The legal constellation around the prospect of securing a patent is complex, especially when considered internationally. But at its core lies originality: the subject matter to be patented must constitute a demonstrable addition to the repository of everything else conceived beforehand in the lineage of developments in question.

Engineering Patents and Spatial Organization

In addition to chronological innovation maps, an analytical study of patents discloses the niches of invention on which a given discipline has most consistently placed emphasis as much as those remaining somewhat or completely unexplored. In the case of engineering, an examination of patents from the nineteenth century to the present reveals a number of central categories.

their purposes, scope, laws, international developments, and trends, see Stephen L. Keefe, "Civil Engineering and Patent Law Blog," https://www.keefeip.com/civil-engineering-and-patent-law. Accessed June 16, 2021. For a brief overview of the civil engineering patent system and history in the US as well as a few patent examples, see Christopher A. Rothe, "Using Patents To Advance The Civil Engineering Profession," in *Civil Engineering Magazine* 76, no. 6 (June 2006): 66–73. More generally, for a lucid and precise introductory account of the patent system in the US, see Craig Allen Nard, "History and Architecture of the Patent Systems," in *The Law of Patents* (New York: Aspen Publishers, 2008), 1–48.

2. See "Patentability Requirements," https://www.epo.org/law-practice/legal-texts/html/guidelines/e/g_i_1.htm. Accessed July 1, 2021.

3. See under "Novelty And Non-Obviousness, Conditions For Obtaining A Patent," https://www.uspto.gov/patents/basics/general-information-patents. Accessed June 29, 2021.

The most significant of these encompasses components and methods used in structural design. From the early advances in reinforced concrete patented by Joseph Monier and François Hennebique over the last few decades of the nineteenth century, to Ildefonso Sánchez del Río's 1954 single curved, reinforced brick vault; from the patents involving prestressed concrete obtained by Eugène Freyssinet in the late 1920s (fig. 8.1), to Frei Otto's 1961 tent roof (fig. 8.2); from Pier Luigi Nervi's 1949 isostatic floor, to the Bubble System AG that Heinz Isler and his collaborators sought to register in 1976—patents here include beams, slabs, columns, walls, and other structural members along with construction systems, details, processes, and techniques. A second category consists of inventions pertaining to material science, for example, Joseph Aspdin's Portland Cement, patented in 1824, and Eduardo Torroja's adiathermic concrete, in 1928. Machinery can be identified as a third genre of patents, spanning anything from concrete mixers to cabins for hydraulic shovels. Lastly, the category under which modeling and calculation systems are found; from numerous patents developed around finite element methods, to computational analysis and BIM.

There is one salient trend that these categories evince: the structural engineering patents germane to the materialization of buildings have primarily engaged the aspect of form concerning new constructional possibilities. There is another aspect of form that appears to have been largely neglected, namely that concerning spatial organization and a number of related aspects such as configuration, arrangement, and disposition. These define the boundary conditions for a series of human activities to be housed within a bounded region of space at the building scale. More precisely, form involves organization in a two-fold sense. On the one hand, it comprises the three-dimensional material set of elements that makes up a building's primary internal armature or ensemble, prior to the introduction of secondary partitions.[4] Form,

4. This primary armature or ensemble, I have come to call *spatial infrastructure*. For more on the epistemology around this newly coined term, see previous essay here. Although sometimes spatial infrastructure and load-bearing framework are one and the same (e.g., at Mansilla + Tuñón's Castilla and León Museum of Contemporary Art in León, Spain), they do not always necessarily coincide. At FOA's Yokohama Terminal, for example, the material construct embodying the building's primary spatial organization is a continuous, nondirectional surface—encompassing bifurcating paths, flat open areas, and smooth transitions between levels—which is not itself the primary load-bearing structure. Rather, this surface is held in place by a discrete, bi-directional assemblage of transversal ribs and longitudinal girders.

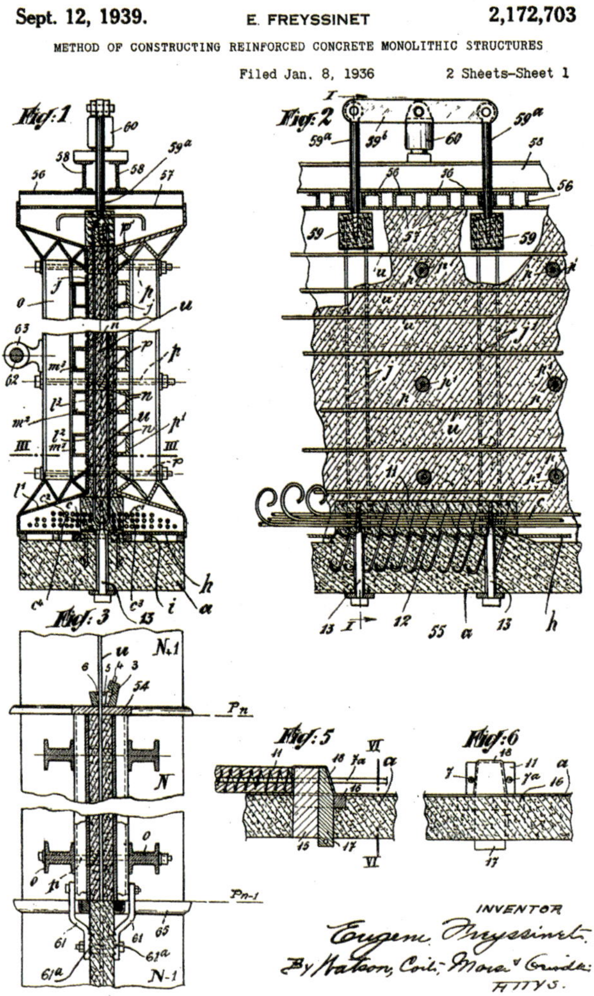

8.1 Eugène Freyssinet. Patent for a “Method of Constructing Reinforced Concrete Monolithic Structures.” US Patent no. 2,172,703. Registered on September 12, 1939.

June 13, 1961 F. OTTO 2,988,096

TENT-ROOF

Filed March 7, 1958

Fig.1

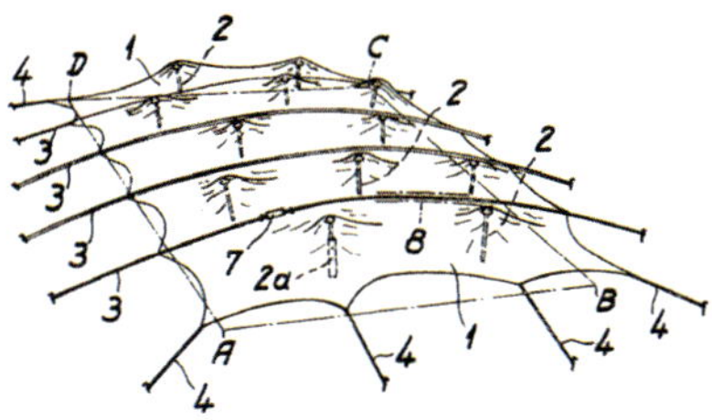

Fig.2

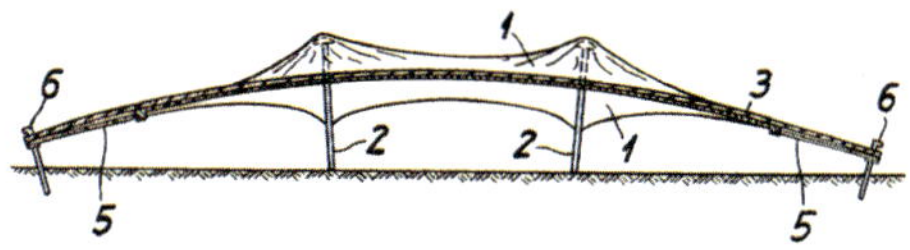

INVENTOR.
FREI OTTO

BY K. A. Mayr.
ATTORNEY.

8.2 Frei Otto. Patent for a "Tent-Roof." US Patent no. 2,988,096. Registered on June 13, 1961.

therefore, *embodies* the very organization of those elements. On the other hand, that three-dimensional ensemble generates a first series of subvolumes of programmable space ordered in a manner linked to—but not coincidental with—its material elements. Form *begets* a specific organization of space.

A study of patents begins to suggest a tendency whereby structural engineering has contributed much innovation in terms of constructional possibilities, while it has failed to substantially expand beyond a reduced number of spatial modalities. Indeed, these have mainly included the single, shed-like space; some version of the large-span roof (pleated surfaces, shells, etc.); variations of the old basilica (i.e., configurations in parallel naves); and more generally, open layouts punctuated by columns. Even the engineering thinking behind the work of notable figures on the edge between architecture and engineering, like Nervi, Eladio Dieste, and Santiago Calatrava, is essentially restricted to the sculptural gesture or external envelope, rather than aiming at the internal arrangement of space.

While the vast majority of structural engineering patents have engaged one aspect of form, there are exceptions, albeit rare and with a marked limitation. Take August Komendant's 1980 patent for a "modular, multi-floor building." It lays out a system of rectangular semi-boxes—no floor and no ceiling, just four walls—which are concrete-cast as rigid units. These semi-boxes are meant to be placed in between concrete slabs and further bound together by post-tensioned tendons running through walls and slabs. There is certainly spatial organization involved here, that is to say that of the semi-boxes engendering a series of spaces both inside them and in between. However, it is not the patent's focus. It is, rather, only a consequence of an invention otherwise motivated by criteria centered around construction methods and load-bearing capabilities, as the objects of the invention make it clear: "suitable for locations which are subjected to severe dynamic forces," "can be erected quickly and inexpensively," "molds can be used more efficiently," "structural units can be handled with relatively low-capacity construction equipment," etc.[5] No wonder there are no floor plans on the patent document. The range of sectional and layout variability seems quite limited as tendons and walls are dependent upon each other and alignment in section is required for the

5. See under "Objects of the Invention," US Patent no. 4,195,453 registered on April 1, 1980.

tendons to maintain vertical continuity. In other words, the semi-boxes ought to be stacked on top of one another in between the floor slabs, which are prescribed as horizontal. Le Corbusier's Maison Dom-Ino propounded a spatial organization where a pile of horizontal slabs is held apart by vertical supports. Essentially, the dispositional logic implicit in Komendant's patent is not so different, and perhaps more restraining. From this standpoint, his 1980 invention takes us back to 1914.

In the minority of structural engineering patents where spatial organization is manifestly present, it is predominantly so as a by-product of other concerns. Architects, on the other hand, have shown an inclination to patent inventions where spatial organization does appear as a primary subject matter. Their scope is, however, rather narrow too. Consider the following series of representative patents by architects: a typical iron skyscraper where a novelty is introduced as to how the stairs are arranged in plan within the vertical core area, with most of the efforts otherwise devoted to construction and fireproofing issues;[6] a multi-story building in which the floor slabs alternately rotate around a central axis containing a vertical core, with all floor slabs otherwise horizontal and equidistant from one another;[7] a non-elevator low-rise residential building, with conventionally stacked units, that offers a ground floor laid out so that it is easily disabled- or handicapped-accessible;[8] a "loft-city" concept by which double height, horizontal floors are repetitively piled up to form a building of indeterminate height and program, one where freedom of horizontal and vertical partition is suggested within each level;[9] a housing building devised around a central core and equidistant structural floor slabs where variability exists at the level of secondary horizonal and vertical partitions within the duplexes that repetitively fill up the envelope;[10] a scheme comprising a multi-story housing building on top of a podium holding a garage which, articulated around stacked horizontal floors equidistant from one another, makes a number of modest contributions in terms of parking

6. US Patent no. 383,170 (reg. on May 22, 1888).

7. US Patent no. 3,226,889 (reg. on Jan. 4, 1966).

8. US Patent no. 6,079,171 (reg. on June 27, 2000).

9. US Patent no. 2005/0086874 (reg. on Apr. 28, 2005).

10. European Patent no. 1 273 741 B1 (reg. on Sep. 26, 2007).

spaces and circulation in addition to details concerning apartment access and service rooms;[11] a system of vertically stacked dwelling or commercial units for both low-rise and high rise construction which, relying on regularly distributed load-bearing walls and conventional layouts, allows for different volumetric configurations within the boundaries set by parallel horizontal floors as well as more or less hackneyed split-level and double-height conditions.[12] The pattern emerging in these and many other similar patents is one where no innovation occurs at the level of the building's essential spatial organization—its primary three-dimensional material ensemble—yet only regarding particular layout details, vertical and horizontal partitions, accessibility, circulation, and modularity. Not unlike the tendency detected in structural engineering patents, no radically novel alternatives concerning models of spatial organization at the building scale are found among patents by architects. Restricted by a proclivity to prioritizing basic functional considerations, those have remained within the confines of a few spatial modalities, often gravitating around the Dom-Ino scheme and its derivatives.

Articulating a Subdomain of the Architecture-Engineering Hybrid

A synthesis of these diagnoses makes it plain that to address the aspect of form generally overlooked in the culture of engineering, efforts ought to focus on spatial organization and do so on the grounds of engineering's scientific thinking. Through the harnessing of systems, the implementation of more and more sophisticated analytical models, and an emphasis on rule-based judgments rooted in logic and mathematics, an epistemology around the establishment of scientific grounds on which to base design practice and research channeled an understanding of the new technologies emerging in the post-war decades—such as those involving information, computers, and artificial intelligence—no longer with a view to problem-solving alone, but also with respect to their synthetic, projective capabilities. As a consequence of this shift, breaking down formal processes into their smallest sets of constituents

11. US Patent no. 7,497,055 (reg. on Mar. 3, 2009).

12. US Patent no. 2017/0362814 A1 (reg. on Dec. 21, 2017).

gained tremendous precision, which in turn allowed such processes to incorporate a much greater degree of complexity in terms of the relationships between those constituents. Mobilizing the inheritance of this epistemology with today's tools has an enormous potential for the conception of new models of spatial organization at the building scale.

To work in that direction, there is one tradition bred by the intersection of science and architecture that is particularly relevant: that of *the architecture-engineering hybrid.*[13] During the period subsequent to Jean-Nicolas-Louis Durand's teachings and all through the nineteenth century, much of what Giedion famously termed "new" architecture (that triggered by the industrial revolution) came about as a result of significant cross-pollinations between the two fields. Paxton's Crystal Palace of 1851 and Barlow's St. Pancras Station of 1868, both in London; Dutert's Gallerie des Machines in Paris of 1889; Tony Garnier's La Mouche in Lyon of 1914; Freyssinet's hangar in Orly of 1923; or the modernist factories designed by engineers such as Owen Williams, Giacomo Matté-Trucco, and Marco Zanuso can be cited here as representative examples of that "new" architecture.[14] Yet the advances brought about by the coming together of architecture and engineering, in these and similar instances, translated primarily into a fascination with either large spans or the emerging constructional possibilities enabled first by iron and glass and later by concrete. One would be hard pressed to find radical alternatives to received models of intricate spatial organizations for hosting human activities in those decades of "new" architecture in the Giedion sense.

It is rather over the second half of the twentieth century that a relatively small subdomain within the tradition of the architecture-engineering hybrid

13. The term "architecture-engineering hybrid" relates to Antoine Picon's "hybrid architect engineer." See Antoine Picon, *Hybrid(e). Marc Mimram: Hybride Architecte Ingénieur = Hybrid Architect Engineer* (Gollion: In folio, 2007). While Picon referred to the figure of one particular hybrid architect-engineer, here a different term is used to more generally allude to a design domain at the intersection of the two disciplines and to suggest implications at an epistemological level.

14. Giedion dated the birth of a "new" kind of industrial architecture to around the year 1830. See Sigfried Giedion, *Building in France, Building in Iron, Building in Ferroconcrete*, Texts & Documents (Santa Monica, CA: Getty Center for the History of Art and the Humanities, 1995), 86.

can be identified, which shows an as yet largely untapped, immense potential to offer those alternatives. This subdomain of design and research can be defined along two axes that clearly distinguish its modus operandi within that entire tradition. First, it exploits some of the core engineering inclinations laid out above—such as the central role of math and geometry, a marked physical empiricism, the importance of procedural thinking, the interpretation of the organizational laws of nature in terms of design, and a focused intensity devoted to the artifact itself—on the basis of their attunement to yielding architectural outcomes, with their distinctive intricacy and relational properties.[15] Second, it capitalizes on the extraordinary power of those inclinations to facilitate the conception of the kinds of patterns, rules, and codifiable gestures that spawn the unmistakable singularity of models of spatial organization in architecture featuring true newness.

Upon closely examining the tradition around the architecture-engineering hybrid, many engineers emerge who ventured into architecture. Yet very few can be claimed to pertain to the subdomain of design and research outlined above. On one side are engineers whose production in architecture limited itself to two fundamentally engineering themes: the shed and certain version of the large-span roof. Isler and Félix Candela, for example, would fall into this category. There are others whose design approach may be considered as both architectural and engineering, but not as *hybrid*. They certainly operated in both architecture and engineering, but they faced architectural scenarios with the conventional design approach of an architect, and engineering scenarios with the approach of an engineer. As a result, their architectural work did not differ substantially from that which could have been conceived by an architect. This category includes figures like Marc Mimram, whose resi-

15. The complexity of functions and activities to be housed in a building (say, a museum or a school, relative to a bridge or a dam) gives rise to the characteristic intricacy and relational properties of architectural form in contradistinction to those of engineering form. With the exception of a building's load-bearing structure—an engineering form to be sure, but one featuring a distinctive internal three-dimensionality determined by architecture's inhabitability—engineering forms such as roads, shells, and roof structures lack the same degree of intricacy in their unfolding, even when they do so three-dimensionally. Frei Otto's membranes and Heinz Isler's sheds come to mind as relevant examples: their organizational intricacy is practically negligible even when compared to that embodied in a simple single-family house. Fundamental differences in degree and kind of organizational intricacy distinguish architectural form from engineering form.

dential projects on the Barbès and Jaurès boulevards, for instance, can only be judged as rather commonplace buildings. A third group comprises names like Nervi, Dieste, and Calatrava. Their architecture features clear traces of an engineering attitude towards design. But, as mentioned above, these traces do not appear to have any significant impact on the internal arrangement of space; only at the level of sculptural gesture or external envelope (fig. 8.3). Unlike that of Isler and Candela, the production of the hybrid subdomain delineated here transcends the typically engineering typologies; unlike Mimram's, its outcomes are indissolubly linked to the engineering-inflected design attributes through which they were begotten; unlike Nervi, Dieste, and Calatrava, the design thinking at its core tackles the internal spatial intricacy characteristic of architectural form, beyond questions concerning the envelope.

Protagonists in this subdomain are not necessarily architect-engineers in any customary sense. Rather, it is the ensemble of their work which, embodying a three-dimensionality characteristic of the nature, purview, and scale of architecture, is here interpreted as establishing an important subdomain in the tradition of the architecture-engineering hybrid. One such protagonist worth mentioning is the Israeli geometer, architect, and engineer Michaël Burt. His body of work, chiefly grounded in structural and theoretical morphology, proves to be one of the earliest and most thoroughgoing investigations into the discovery and visualization of models for the subdivision of space based on patterns of configurational continuity. The American physicist and computer scientist Alan Schoen can be added as someone also operating around morphology. He developed a large number of two-dimensional tiling patterns and infinite, triply periodic minimal surfaces. Engineer and theorist Cecil Balmond is a further example. He is an early and one of the few translators of aspects of nonlinearity and algorithmic reasoning into design moves of significant architectural consequence, contributing applications of design frameworks thus initiated to the conception of entire buildings (i.e., beyond small pavilions, facades, and pieces of furniture). Taken together, the production and design thinking constituting this subdomain point to fundamentally new ways of organizing space at the building scale and come to relate to a critical twenty-first-century phenomenon: an ever-closer rapport between

8.3 Eladio Dieste and Eugenio Montañez, Citricos Caputto Fruit Packing Plant in Salto, Uruguay (1971–1972).

architecture and engineering, and the ever-growing presence of scientifically minded designers in architecture that comes with it.[16]

One central characteristic of the hybrid approach of figures like Burt and Balmond is a *two-fold structural awareness*. In synthesizing elements pertaining to the logic of a building's physical support and the organizational traits of form, such two-fold structural awareness catalyzes a productive link between the feasibility of a three-dimensional physical frame and its aptness to housing a set of human activities. By "productive link" two things are meant. First, wherever there is one principal logic governing both of those aspects of an architectural configuration, an efficiency of design thinking results that would be absent if two separate logics were required—efficiency that is usually favored from an engineering standpoint. Second, turning properties and laws typically associated with the engineering control of a three-dimensional physical frame into a generative spatial code in certain specific ways can push the bounds of possibility of architectural configurations. Procedures to that effect may involve a veiled coextension of force and spatial organization (in contrast to either the total neglect of force, or the typical determinism of form-finding processes) or exploiting the pliable systematicity inherent to differentiated patterns of form-generation.

Niche of Opportunity

Should inventions arisen out of the hybrid subdomain put forward here be registered, they would come to fill a historical gap in the legacy of engineering patents by engaging the aspect of form involving spatial organization. Notably, some of Burt's and Schoen's abstract geometric models describing spatial arrangements realistically capable of housing a set of human activities could be interpreted as bases for buildings. They would have to be worked out both structurally and architecturally in some detail, with a view to patenting them on grounds of their overall functional performance as well as their internal (re-)configurability, flexibility, and spatial possibilities. Some of Balmond's design methods articulated simultaneously around, on the one hand, nume-

16. In many ways, this phenomenon represents a logical evolution of the shift toward an acute scientization of design that has been unfolding across developed countries since WWII.

rically or geometrically controlled sequences of order, unfolding patterns, and rule sets, and on the other an understanding of structural performance, could be patented in relation to the specific class of spatial arrangements they generate. As could his variations on the Vierendeel beam along with its compositional capabilities to originate a building holding a series of alternating inhabitable interiors and big voids.

As references for registering inventions of that sort, there are a few exceptions to the tendencies identified above in engineering and architectural patents which, though lacking in organizational variability as presented, are nonetheless quite informative. For example, a 1970 patent proposes a high-rise building made up of individual houses that are arrayed on a checkerboard pattern around a cylinder void (fig. 8.4);[17] a scheme registered in 2006 combines a set of three-dimensionally staggered apartments into one coherent volume.[18] Another relevant reference is OMA's "Patent Office," a series of patent abstracts laying out concepts rooted in spatial manipulations and subversions under the rubric of "Universal Modernization Patent"—abstracts which obviously would have to be rigorously developed to measure up to patentability standards.[19]

Far from being an end in itself, seeking to address the aspect of form that has been the least probed in engineering's historical process of scientization is a project justified by scientific thinking's unique capacity to facilitate the conception of new models of spatial organization at the building scale. And engaging scientific thinking in a manner different from that reflected in engineering's patent history happens to be intrinsic to that project.

17. US Patent no. 3,535,835 (reg. on Oct. 27, 1970).

18. European Patent no. 1 455 033 B2 (reg. on Jan. 4, 2006).

19. Rem Koolhaas and AMO/OMA, "Patent Office," in *Content* (Cologne: Taschen, 2004), 73–83, 510–13.

8.4 “House of Houses” by Josef Küpper, a model of which is here depicted in October 1964. The concept was patented in 1970 as “Detached Building Units on Plural Support Platforms.”

Acknowledgments

This book is the result of years of intensely probing fundamental questions in and around the domain of architectural thinking through writing, teaching, designing, and various forms of public speaking engagements. I am grateful to the numerous commentators—critics, audience members, online and email interlocutors, respondents, editors, friends, and colleagues—who raised relevant issues concerning the nature, reach, complexity, potential, history, boundaries, contradictions, and richness of this domain of knowledge. There are more of them than I can remember today. Stan Allen, Penelope Dean, Kenneth Frampton, Sanford Kwinter, Sylvia Lavin, Mary Mcleod, John McMorrough, Bryan Norwood, Etien Santiago, and Enrique Walker had the most palpable impact on the content presented here. My own students at Columbia and Cornell made invaluable contributions to my thinking about this material.

To all of those who showed an interest in publishing some of these essays in the past, much gratitude is owed. I would like to thank Ricardo Devesa for taking on this project and for his wisdom throughout, as well as our outstanding team at Actar—Marga Gibert for her talent and care with the text and design, and Lorena Lozano and Camila Joaqui for their commitment, precision, and reliability. Sonia Hill has been the best copy editor I could possibly have hoped for. Working on this project with such an extraordinary group of professionals has been both delightful and extremely enriching on all levels.

For their unwavering support, this book is dedicated to my parents and my sister.

— José Aragüez
Paris, June 2022

Index

Author Biography

José Aragüez, PhD, is a licensed practicing architect heading José Aragüez Architects, an office for architecture and urbanism based in Paris, New York, and Málaga. He is also a writer and an educator, having led graduate studios and seminars at Columbia University from 2013–20 and having held the 2020–21 H. Deane Pearce Endowed Chair at Texas Tech. Aragüez obtained a PhD in the History and Theory of Architecture from Princeton University. Earlier he graduated with a Master of Architecture and Urbanism from the University of Granada, Spain (Honorable Mention, University Graduation Extraordinary Award, and 1st National Prize in Architecture) and, from Columbia GSAPP, with a Post-Professional Master's Degree (Honor Prize for Excellence in Design) and a Graduate Certificate in Advanced Architectural Research. Aragüez has lectured extensively across Europe and North America—including most of the top schools—in addition to the Middle East and Japan. Besides Columbia and Texas Tech, he has taught at Cornell, Princeton, Penn, Rice University in Paris, and the University of Granada. His recent six-year project (2014–19), involving the publication of *The Building* (Lars Müller Publishers, 2016), is widely regarded in international circles as one of the most significant contributions to architectural discourse in the 2010s. His writings have also appeared in *e-flux, Flat Out, European Architecture History Network Proceedings, Pidgin, The Routledge Companion to Criticality in Art, Architecture and Design* (Routledge, 2018), and *Radical Pedagogies* (MIT Press, 2022).

Image Credits

Every effort has been made to supply complete and correct credits; if there are errors or omissions, please contact the publisher so that corrections can be made in any subsequent edition.

Introduction
Fig. 0.1 (p.13): https://www.flickr.com/photos/eager/14049432168. © Creative Commons.

Self-Determinacy via Disciplinary Diversification: The Cooper Union School of Architecture, 1964–1985
Fig. 1.1 (p. 18): Photograph by Daniel Libeskind. Courtesy of The Irwin S. Chanin School of Architecture Archive of The Cooper Union.
Fig. 1.2 (p. 21): John Hejduk, *Mask of Medusa: Works, 1947–1983* (New York: Rizzoli, 1985), 37–38. © John Hejduk.
Fig. 1.3 (p. 24–25): Photographer unknown. Courtesy of The Irwin S. Chanin School of Architecture Archive of The Cooper Union.
Fig. 1.4 (p. 33): Photographs by Jean-Michel Crettaz. Courtesy of The Irwin S. Chanin School of Architecture Archive of The Cooper Union.
Fig. 1.5 (p. 36–37): Photographer unknown. Courtesy of The Irwin S. Chanin School of Architecture Archive of The Cooper Union.

Toward a Critique of "The Organic" in Architectural Thinking
Essay first published in *Pidgin*, no. 12 (Spring 2012), 246–63.
Fig. 2.1 (p. 46–47): Peter Blundell-Jones, *Hans Scharoun* (London: Phaidon Press, 1995), 104–05. © Peter Blundell-Jones.
Fig. 2.2 (p. 51): Antonio Juárez, *El Universo Imaginario De Louis I. Kahn* (Colección Arquithesis. Barcelona, Spain: Fundación Caja de arquitectos, 2006), 124. © Antonio Juárez.
Fig. 2.3 (p. 52): Fumihiko Maki, *Nurturing Dreams: Collected Essays on Architecture and the City* (Cambridge, MA: MIT Press, 2008), 46, 62. © Fumihiko Maki.

The Building's Discursive Building
Essay first published in José Aragüez, ed., *The Building* (Zürich: Lars Müller Publishers, 2016), 10–19.

Sponge territory
Essay first published in *Flat Out*, no. 2 (Fall 2017), 3, 32–36.
Fig. 4.1 (p. 70): © Hisao Suzuki
Fig. 4.2 (p. 72): © Lucas K. Doolan, Studio Mikkspace.
Fig. 4.3 (p. 73): © Lucas K. Doolan, Studio Mikkspace.
Fig. 4.4 (p. 79): © Lucas K. Doolan, Studio Mikkspace.

On Architecture's Metacriticality
Essay first published in Chris Bisbin and Myra Thiessen, eds., *The Routledge Companion to Criticality in Art, Architecture and Design* (London: Routledge, 2018), 167–78.

Critical Imageability
Essay first published in *e-Flux architecture* (Fall 2018), https://www.e-flux.com/

architecture/positions/222387/critical-imageability.
Fig. 6.1 (p. 106): Deyan Sudjic, *Future Systems* (New York, NY: Phaidon, 2006), 208. © Deyan Sudjic.
Fig. 6.2 (p. 108): *Hunch, the Berlage Institut report No. 11,* (Amsterdam, The Netherlands: Episode Publishers, 2007), 33
Fig. 6.3 (p. 110): minoa.eu, and Divisare, respectively.
Fig. 6.4 (p. 112): Foreign Office Architects and Institute of Contemporary Arts (London, England), *Phylogenesis: Foa's Ark* (Barcelona, Spain: Actar, 2003), 505.
Fig. 6.5 (p. 118–119): *Zodiac*, no. 16 (1966), 141–42.
Fig. 6.6 (p. 120–121): Igor Marjanović, *Marina City: Bertrand Goldberg's Urban Vision* (New York, NY: Princeton Architectural Press, 2010), 53. © Igor Marjanović.
Fig. 6.7 (p. 122): Germano Celant, Herzog & de Meuron, and Fondazione Prada (Milan, Italy), eds., *Prada Aoyama Tokyo: Herzog & de Meuron*, 2. ed (Milan: Fondazione Prada, 2003), 103. © Germano Celant, Herzog & de Meuron, and Fondazione Prada.
Fig. 6.8 (p. 124): EU Mies Award (http://www.miesarch.com/work/1683). © Norman Foster.
Fig. 6.9 (p. 125): Enrique Sobejano, Fuensanta Nieto, and Ana Pascual Posada, *Nieto Sobejano – Memory and Invention* (Ostfildern, Germany: Hatje Cantz, 2013), 230. © Enrique Sobejano, Fuensanta Nieto, and Ana Pascual Posada.

Spatial Infrastructure
Fig. 7.1 (p. 130): Fondation Le Corbusier, http://www.fondationlecorbusier.fr/corbuweb/morpheus.aspx?sysId=13&IrisObjectId=5972&sysLanguage=en-en&itemPos=102&itemCount=215&sysParentId=65&sysParentName=home. © F.L.C. / ADAGP, Paris / Artists Rights Society (ARS), New York 2022.
Fig. 7.2 (p. 135): Mansilla+Tuñón. © Luis Asín
Fig. 7.3 (p. 138–139): FOA, Alejandro Zaera-Polo. © Alejandro Zaera-Polo.
Fig. 7.4 (p. 140): OMA: https://www.oma.com/projects/jussieu-two-libraries. © Hans Werlemann.
Fig. 7.5 (p. 149): © Hisao Suzuki.

Patenting Arrangement
Fig. 8.1 (p. 154): United States Patent and Trademark Office. © Public Domain.
Fig. 8.2 (p. 155): United States Patent and Trademark Office. © Public Domain.
Fig. 8.3 (p. 162): © Julián Palacio
Fig. 8.4 (p. 165): https://www.alamy.com/oct-10-1964-a-house-of-houses-has-been-created-by-architect-josef-image69412874.html. © Alamy.

Spatial Infrastructure
Essays on Architectural Thinking as a Form of Knowledge

Published by
Actar Publishers, New York, Barcelona
www.actar.com

Author/Editor
José Aragüez

Copyediting and proofreading
Sonia Hill

Printing and binding
Arlequin, Barcelona

This publication is made possible in part by a grant from the Barr Ferree Foundation Fund for Publications, Department of Art and Archaeology, Princeton University.

Distribution
Actar D, Inc. New York, Barcelona.

New York
440 Park Avenue South, 17th Floor
New York, NY 10016, USA
T +1 2129662207
salesnewyork@actar-d.com

Barcelona
Roca i Batlle 2
08023 Barcelona, Spain
T +34 933 282 183
eurosales@actar-d.com

Indexing
English ISBN: 978-1-63840-019-6
Library of Congress Control Number: 2022932949

Printed in Spain

Publication date: September 2022